# THE COLLECTOR'S BOOK OF ENGLISH COUNTRY POTTERY

BY THE SAME AUTHOR

*The English Country Pottery: Its History and Techniques*

# THE COLLECTOR'S BOOK OF ENGLISH COUNTRY POTTERY

Peter C. D. Brears



DAVID & CHARLES
NEWTON ABBOT LONDON
NORTH POMFRET (VT) VANCOUVER

0 7153 6495 2



Set in 11/13pt Baskerville and printed in Great Britain for David & Charles (Holdings) Limited South Devon House Newton Abbot Devon

Published in the United States of America by David & Charles Inc North Pomfret Vermont 05053 USA

Published in Canada by Douglas David & Charles Limited 3645 McKechnie Drive West Vancouver BC

# *Contents*

# *List of Illustrations*

## *Plates*

## *In Text*

# *Introduction*

It is a strange phenomenon that English collectors have always admired the everyday ceramic productions of distant countries while entirely neglecting those of their own. The majority of large private or public collections in England contain a wealth of imported wares, ranging from the painted amphorae of the ancient Greeks to the glazed stonewares of the medieval Japanese, but few indeed possess good examples of native English peasant pottery. Were these traditional wares of a poor standard, this neglect could be easily understood, but with their robust forms, their fine sense of proportion and their technical excellence they are in many respects of an unparalleled quality. Other types of pottery may well exceed them in their standards of manufacture and contrived aesthetic appeal, but it is not for these accomplishments that these wares are best known. Being the products of a full-blooded peasant society they form an inimitable combination of sound design, material economy and fitness of purpose which, almost incidentally, has created some extremely beautiful examples of ceramic art. In many continental countries wares of this type have been collected and studied for many years, a number of extremely well-illustrated volumes being produced recently. Some of these have even been re-published in English editions, so that it is now easier for English collectors to read of the wares of rural Spain than of those of their own country.[1] If this book only slightly corrects this strange imbalance, it will have achieved much of its purpose.

The main aim of this volume is to present a detailed

account of the country pottery made in England during the last two hundred years. This particular period of its history is of great interest to the collector, for it represents the final flowering of the peasant potter's craft before his products were entirely replaced by factory-made wares. It also represents a period for which there is a wealth of appropriate documentation, thus enabling us to study not only the individual pots themselves, but also the various local customs and traditions associated with their usage. Further, there are still many excellent examples of this type of ware to be purchased for a matter of a few pounds at the most in the numerous market stalls, junk shops and antique shops which lie scattered throughout most parts of the country.

When commencing a collection it is well to remember that country pottery is essentially household ware, and that even today it often comes into the saleroom or shop directly from the house where it was in everyday use for many years. This fact is particularly important, for the value of this type of pottery often lies in its history, or provenance, and not merely in the state of the pot or in the mark impressed upon its base. To acquire a fine hen and chickens money box, for example, may give considerable satisfaction, but how much more so if it is known that it was made for James Whitaker, the schoolmaster of Kendal in Westmorland, who ordered it from a potter from Burton-in-Lonsdale who was attending the Kendal Fair of 1834. Similarly a milk jug would become immeasurably more interesting if its owner knew that it had been used last century by Mrs Smith at Wood Farm, Newton. This information is often readily available if inquiries are tactfully made through the respective auctioneers or dealers, and must be obtained if at all possible. It is usually a good plan to record both the place and date of purchase, together with any details regarding the history of the pot, on the actual base of the pot itself. If this is done in Indian ink and is protected by a thin smear of clear varnish or lacquer, the information will be perfectly safe, no matter how many times the pot is washed. Separate notes or paper labels, however firmly tied on, are not to be recommended, as they have an alarming habit of becoming separated from their respective pots.

Fortunately, the care of country pottery presents but few problems for the collector, for although it may be broken, its materials are otherwise of an almost indestructible nature. Even so, a few words of advice on its treatment may prevent some unfortunate accidents. As the earthenware from which these pots are made is essentially a porous substance, it is unwise to use it for the prolonged storage of liquids. Water, for example, will slowly find its way beneath the protective glaze and may eventually cause the glaze itself to peel off. Tea will stain any cracks with its tannin, while home-made wines will cause the glaze to decompose, ruining the pot and poisoning the collector with its high lead content. Extremes of heat and cold should also be avoided, for an old stew pot can easily crack when lifted from a hot oven, as can a flower pot left out overnight in the frost. Normally a quick wash in warm soapy water, followed by a clean rinse and a final drying with a soft cloth, is all that is necessary to bring a pot up to a perfect finish. Abrasives, or the use of a knife or scraper, should never be resorted to, as they will inflict permanent scars on the pot's surface. If there should be any splashes of tar or paint on the vessel it is usually best to leave them in place, as they are often quite meaningful, and add considerably to the interest and character of the piece. A smear of tar on a farm labourer's bottle, for example, could point to its use when the sheep were being salved in the autumn, while an inch-thick layer of paint inside a deep bowl might indicate its use by a wheelwright, hand-grinding his own colours with linseed oil. It would be a mistake to remove any accretions of this type, but stains of a more recent nature may be removed by the use of a commercial paint stripper, which involves carefully wiping off the softened paint with soft cloths or tissues.

However carefully pottery is handled, breakages are bound to occur sooner or later, and the immediate instinct is to find the nearest tube of the strongest possible glue and to stick the pieces back together once more. This can be extremely dangerous, for many of today's glues are far stronger than the materials they join, so that a single error in joining may prove impossible to correct. The only 'safe' glue to use is clear balsa cement, which is strong enough to hold any pot in shape, but which may be dissolved again or cleaned off with the application of a little acetone or nail-polish remover. Using this adhesive, pottery of any type may be repaired with confidence, for no permanent damage can be done. If you follow these simple methods it should be possible to preserve some superb examples of traditional craftsmanship for the future while still giving great pleasure to those who see them today.

*Note for the Introduction is on page 177*

## *Chapter One*

# *The Development of the Craft*

Pottery vessels have played an important part in our everyday domestic life from prehistoric times through to the present day, providing us with vessels to cook and wash in, to eat from, to store food in, or to satisfy us with their appearance alone. Obviously the forms and functions of the various pots made in England over the last five thousand years have developed considerably as they reflected the changing needs of an evolving society. From the earliest periods up to the final decline of the country potteries, however, these wares had certain definite qualities in common. Firstly, they were made entirely with the purely natural raw materials which the potter found ready to hand in his own locality, the clay requiring only the crudest cleaning and preparation before being used. Secondly, they were made by a man who formed an essential element of his native society, who knew that society and its requirements intimately, and who was thus able to produce the precise forms of vessel which it required. Thirdly, they were made by a skilled and sensitive craftsman who, due to a lifetime of handling clay and a sound background of traditional practice, could produce an unmistakable balance of good form, functional shape and technical excellence. It is clear that a far larger volume than this would be required to trace the full history of the hand-made pottery industry of England, but most of the extant evidence is already in print for the archaeologist or the collector to consult. For the later periods, however, most ceramic historians have concentrated on the early eighteenth-century development of factory-made wares, assuming that good quality hand-made wares ceased to be produced in any quantity from this time on. In fact this assumption is quite erroneous, for the English peasant earthenware tradition continued to expand and flourish from the early eighteenth century through to its final decline over the course of the last few decades. The wares made during this period, therefore, form the subject of the present volume.

To place these wares in historical perspective it is perhaps best to trace their development from the late medieval period, noting the various influences which affected their early evolution. The medieval English housewife had relied on a very restricted range of wares for her everyday use, the jug, cooking pot and bowl being the most common vessels, as chafing dishes, three-legged skillets and other specialised items were comparatively rare, being only in occasional use. During the late fifteenth and early sixteenth centuries, however, a variety of new pottery forms became popular as a result of a number of strong continental influences. The most important of these new forms was the individual drinking vessel, or cup. Although cups had been used in England for the greater part of the medieval period, they had always been made of ash wood, being subject therefore to staining, splitting and splintering, which must have made them extremely unpleasant to drink from after prolonged use. In northern Europe pottery cups had been widely used for some time, for the advantages of the strong ceramic fabrics covered in a hard, glossy and easily cleaned glaze were quickly realised there. In Germany and the Netherlands hard-fired stoneware drinking vessels from the Rhineland were extremely common, and it appears likely that they stimulated the production of similar types of vessel in northern England from the late fifteenth century at least. These 'Cistercian wares',[1] as they are now known, were used in most parts of the country north of a line running approximately from Bristol to London. They were characterised by a smooth brown-glazed red fabric finely worked into a range of small cups, mugs and posset pots, the latter having shallow conical lids with pierced knobs to allow the hot steam to rise from their boiling contents. In the counties of southern and eastern England, however, French pottery styles were more frequently adopted, the white clays of west Surrey being formed into green-glazed cups, jugs and chafing dishes which closely followed their French originals. These were the famous Tudor Greenwares, which continued to be made until quite late in the seventeenth century.

A second more potent wave of continental influence spread throughout the country during the late sixteenth century following the arrival of tens of thousands of Protestant Flemings who were fleeing from religious persecution in the Netherlands in the 1560s. The Flemish housewife was enjoying the use of an extremely wide range of kitchen and table wares at this period, as such artists as Pieter Breughel the Elder recorded in his paintings. Even if the refugees did not bring their own pottery with them into England, they would certainly have wanted to use similar wares in their new homes, and would probably have obtained suitable replacements from their local potter. In this way, it is suggested, a great variety of new vessels became accepted into everyday use in England. Certainly by the opening of the seventeenth century such items as pottery plates, pipkins, ointment pots, chamber pots and candlesticks, all carefully following the pattern of Netherlands examples, were being used in the majority of English households. Most of these wares were copied in a buff-coloured clay covered in a warm yellow lead glaze, thus earning themselves the title of Midlands Yellow-wares. Another most important development resulting from this Netherlands influence was the adoption of the continental slip-trailing technique of pottery decoration, which had previously been totally unknown in England. The process of slip-trailing consisted of piping coloured slip (ie liquid clay) through a pierced cow horn on to a piece of half-dry ware, the action being similar to that employed by a confectioner when icing cakes. This gave the potter an extremely rapid, simple and versatile decorative technique which enabled him to produce more attractive and readily saleable wares than ever before.

The greatly enlarged range of wares now made by the potters, coupled with various technical advances, gave the early seventeenth-century pottery industry an unprecedented potential for further expansion, but this could not be achieved without a great reorganisation of its trading practices. Even though some of the major individual customers such as colleges or large noble households might order their pottery directly from the potter, the majority of the selling and distribution was carried out by the potter himself through the local markets. This system had many defects, for if the local clay was poor the local people had to make do with poor-quality wares; if fuel was scarce, the wares were expensive; if the winter was hard, no pots could be made and, as the potters could not afford warehousing facilities, none would be available for sale. About the second quarter of the seventeenth century an efficient marketing system slowly emerged through the services of the pot-mongers, pot-sellers or cratemen. These men acted as merchants, undertaking to buy, transport and sell large quantities of the potter's wares at their own risk. Their activities had a considerable effect on the contemporary pottery trade, since, for the first time, they brought the country's potteries into open competition with one another. Each pottery had to rely on its own resources to survive and, as could be expected, those potteries with the most suitable geological situation and good access to the main trade routes soon began to force their less fortunate competitors out of business. In the southern counties the effects of this new trading system were very slight, for each pottery had much the same resources as its neighbour and, except for the area round London, it was probably futile to arrange a developed marketing system. Thus, due to this lack of change, many of the southern potteries continued to produce their wares in an uninterrupted tradition from the medieval period. In the midlands, however, the new trading practices led to a complete reorganisation and resiting of the pottery industry. The village of Burslem near Newcastle-under-Lyme in Staffordshire possessed the unsurpassable advantages of a unique range of clays, a well-stocked

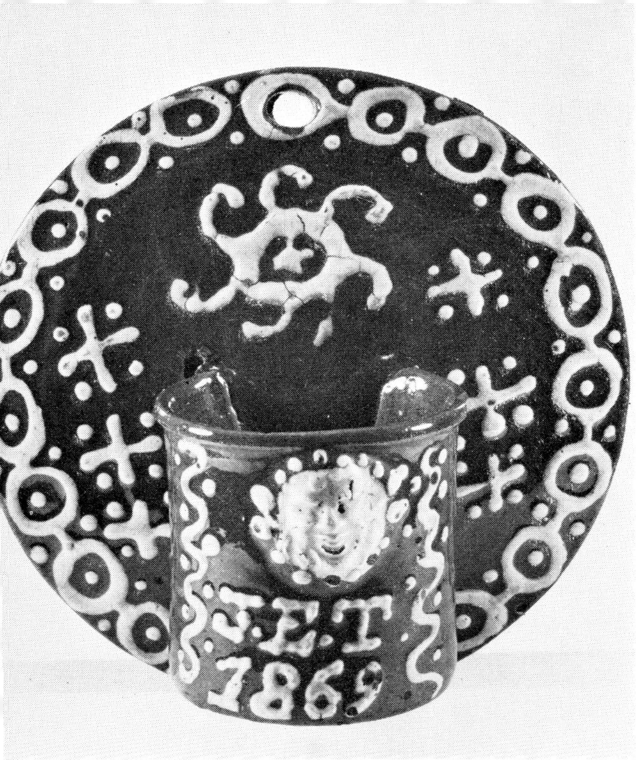

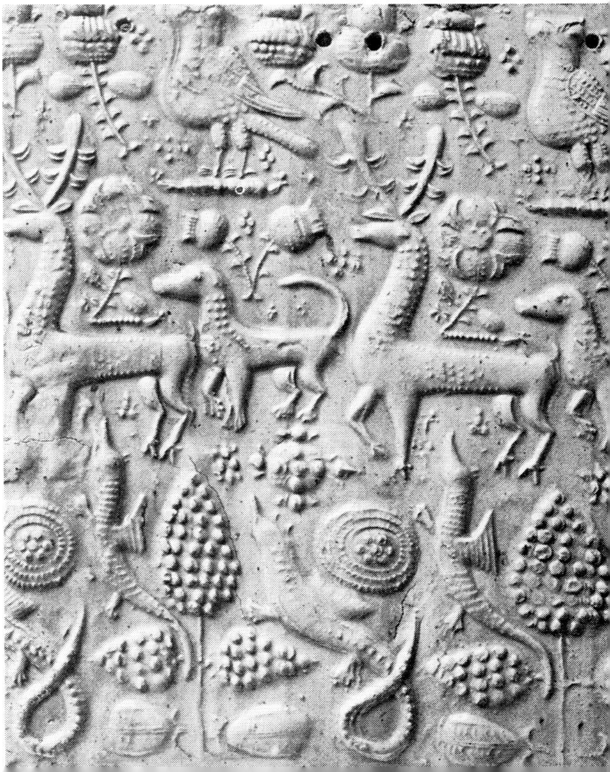

*Page 17* Decorative techniques seen in (*above*) slip-trailing on a Halifax candle holder by Samuel Catherall and (*right*) a roller-decorated tile probably from the Wattisfield Pottery, Suffolk (see notes on page 181)

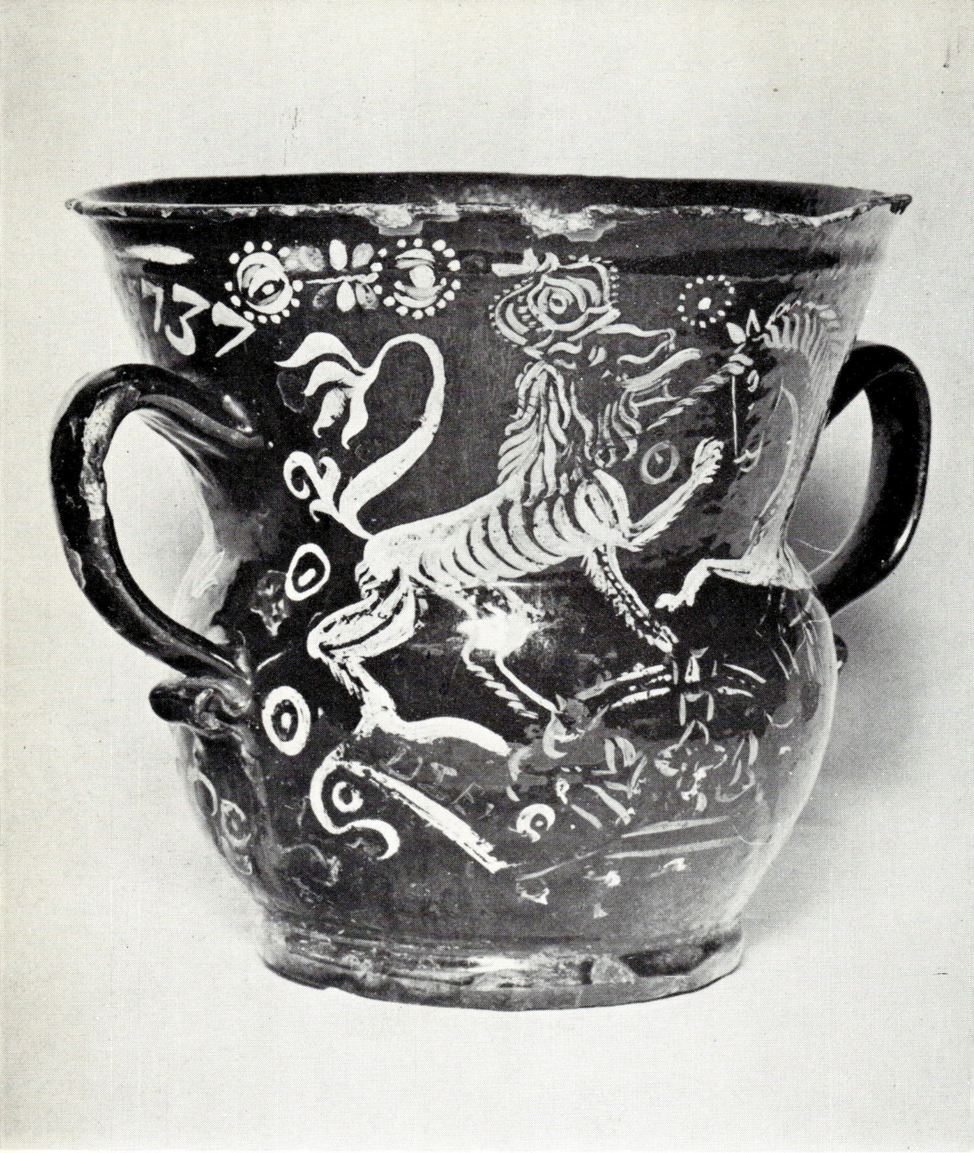

*Page 18* A fine example of early oil-painted decoration, probably made at Bate Hayne, Halifax in 1737 (see notes on page 181)

coalfield and good transport facilities, while its near neighbour, Ticknall, in Derbyshire, had a good supply of clay and coal, an established community of potters and a reasonable situation from which to distribute its produce. Using these advantages to the full, these two potteries began to supply large areas of the midlands, the Burslem wares being distributed by 'poor *crate men,* who carry them at their *backs* all over the *countrey*'[2] while the 'earthen vessels, potts and pancions [made] at Tychnall [were] carried all East England through'.[3] The effects of this considerable expansion in the trading areas of these potteries has recently been emphasised by the discovery of large quantities of Burslem slipwares in a 1652–6 context in Bristol,[4] some 124 miles away, and at Kirkhamgate near Wakefield,[5] 70 miles distant. These finds give conclusive proof of the great areas this pottery was already serving during the mid to late seventeenth century. The ever-growing competition from these new pottery centres was so effective in fact that almost every pottery in Lincolnshire, Cambridgeshire, Leicestershire, Bedfordshire, Oxfordshire and Northamptonshire was forced to close down by the year 1700. As might have been expected, both the Burslem and the Ticknall potteries prospered and grew in size as a result of the increased demand for their wares created by the cratemen etc, and by the close of the seventeenth century some twenty to thirty potteries were already working in Burslem, thus making it the largest and most important pottery-producing centre in England at this surprisingly early date. Having such numbers of potters working together in close proximity appears to have fostered both the growth of specialisation within the trade, as certain individuals concentrated solely on the production of slipware plates, for example, or butter pots, and an increased degree of competition for technical excellence between one potter and another. Competition and specialisation within the industry were also encouraged by the newly acquired habit of tea drinking, for which expensive porcelain and red Yi-Hsing stonewares of extremely high quality were imported by the English and Dutch East India Companies. As early as 1691

John Dwight of Fulham had been granted a patent for the manufacture of 'Transparent Earthenware comonly Knowne by the names of Porcelaine or China . . .', while further effective pseudo-Chinese wares were produced in England by two Dutch potters, John Philip and David Ellers. Their first pottery had been set up in Fulham about 1690, but within the next few years they had removed to Bradwell Wood, a short distance from Burslem, where they made 'ye fine teapotts, cups, and saucers of ye fine red Earth in imitation and as Curious at yt wch comes from China'. To create these extremely competent wares they pioneered the use of the lathe and finely engraved relief moulds in copper which, together with a much more careful method of clay preparation, were entirely new innovations to the Staffordshire pottery industry. Following this lead, neighbouring potters such as Twyford, Astbury and the Wedgwoods began their experiments, each trying to imitate the peerless whiteness and high finish of the imported porcelains. By the use of such new materials as ground calcined flint, Cornish china clay and china stone in the fabrics, and flint glass, zinc oxide and sand in the glaze, they developed entirely new classes of ware which were vastly superior to their common lead-glazed earthenware predecessors. New methods of manufacture too, such as the use of plaster of Paris moulds for slip-casting and copper plates for engraved transfer-printed decoration, all aided the conversion of the potter's craft into an industrial factory-based process. It was now impossible for a single potter to produce fine wares at competitive rates, for he lacked the necessary skill, time, labour, equipment and capital. The making of pottery had now become so complex a process that it could flourish only where large-scale mass-production techniques were adopted to the full. The new wares made by the eighteenth-century Staffordshire potters were of an unprecedented quality, both in their design and in their execution.

At first it might be thought that the rapid expansion of the pottery factories would have completed the collapse of those smaller potteries which had managed to continue working on a cottage-industry basis throughout the rest of the country, but this was not so. Being of such a high standard, the factory products tended to replace the contemporary better-class tableware, which was in pewter. As pewter was rather soft, it required constant attention to remove the knife-cuts it received at table, besides which it was rather unpleasant to eat from. The new ceramic tableware, however, possessed a hard glass-like surface which was easily cleaned, which withstood the action of the knife and fork, and which was decorated in an attractive range of modelled, painted or printed details. Now, as the Staffordshire potteries concentrated almost exclusively on the production of fine earthenware for the upper and middle classes, the less lucrative working-class coarse-wares slowly lapsed into a relatively unimportant position. During the latter half of the eighteenth century a number of major changes in the size and distribution of the population were taking place as the Industrial Revolution progressed. The fertile lands of Cheshire, Norfolk, Suffolk and the southern midlands ceased to be the most populous areas as new industrial regions grew round London, the west midlands, Lancashire, Durham and the West Riding of Yorkshire. The communities which gradually converged towards and expanded round these centres during the latter years of the century were largely composed of wage labourers, many of whom earned hardly enough to support themselves and their families at subsistence level, and so an ever-increasing demand for the cheapest varieties of coarse pottery grew up. To satisfy this demand many new potteries sprang up throughout the country, while most of the old-established ones began a period of slow expansion as they recaptured the trade appropriated from them by the Staffordshire and Derbyshire potters a hundred years before.

The coarse earthenware potteries which worked in England from the mid-eighteenth century onwards derived their styles and ranges of ware from the pottery traditions of their own particular region. In the south and west, where the seventeenth-century competition of Staffordshire had been negligible, the potters had continued to develop particular varieties of ware to suit their local needs. The New Forest pottery of Verwood, for example, still made the coarse yellow-ware costrels in which the farm labourers of all the neighbouring counties carried their ale or cider into the fields. The potteries of central Wiltshire continued to make their dark-glazed jugs and ornate posset pots for use in local festivities, while Donyatt, in the Vale of Taunton Deane, concentrated on puzzle jugs, fuddling cups and other domestic wares, as it had done in the seventeenth century. Further to the west, meanwhile,

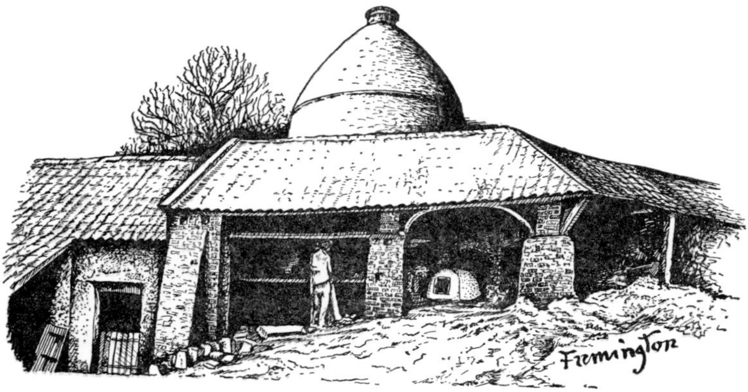


Fig 1 The Fremington Pottery *c.* 1900

the Barnstaple, Fremington and Bideford potters were approaching the peak of their rich sgraffito-ware tradition, which had progressed continuously from the 1550s at least. In the north and the midlands, where the early competition of Staffordshire had been particularly strong, the potters tended to produce wares of a rather more uniform character, using almost the same materials and techniques at each individual kiln. Most of the potters made a fairly limited range of wares, comprising in the main mugs, jugs, bottles, baking bowls and plates, together with a few of the more unusual items such as money boxes, ovens and cradles, but towards the end of the eighteenth century this range was gradually extended as a number of new forms were adopted. The rapidly growing urban populations, clinging to the rural ways of life that they had always known, still prepared much of their own food, salting down their joints of meat and brewing their own beer. To perform these activities a number of large vessels were required which had traditionally been obtained from the cooper, but now the potters competed for and won this considerable market, adding pork, ham and tongue pans, salt jars and huge brewing pots to their repertoire. Similar changes also took place in the provision of dairy equipment for farms and small-holdings, as pottery milk bowls, cream pots, butter pots and milk churns replaced their cooper-made predecessors. A little later, in the opening years of the nineteenth century, the potters began to make further items for purely domestic use, either inventing new vessels to satisfy a particular local need or adapting some of the simpler woodworker's products into ceramic forms. In this way chicken fountains, beetle traps, butter dishes, candle holders, tea caddies and knife boxes came to be made in ever-increasing quantities.

Various forms of horticultural wares also began to play an important part in the potter's trade as the century progressed. Some, such as field-drainage pipes, rhubarb and seakale pots etc, were for strictly utilitarian purposes, reflecting the growing interest in farming and food production, but other types, including ornamental flower pots and vases, were being ordered in large numbers too. Spurred on by lectures at the local church or mechanic's institute, many working men were developing a taste for the popular aspects of the natural sciences, collecting such items as stuffed birds and fishes, dried and pressed seaweeds, flowers or grasses, fossils or bird's eggs, all of which were prominently displayed at home. Live plants, too, in the form of flowers on the window sill, were becoming quite common in even the poorest districts. To house these plants the potters made wide ranges of 'rustic' wares, including such items as bouquet holders, trellis-work flower pot holders, wall pots, rustic épergnes, and fern pots from the 1850s onwards. Most of these wares were executed in a red fabric, the surface of which had been coarsely incised with the prongs of a fork to produce a realistic bark-like finish, often enlivened by the application of a few slip-decorated 'knots'. For the more discerning customer, however, the potter was often prepared to go to great lengths to produce flower pots of a particular design. Many weeks of patient research were frequently necessary before satisfactory results were obtained, as Absolom Harris of the Farnham pottery discovered when he attempted to reproduce some French green-glazed garden vases for Birket Foster, the well-known artist and illustrator.

Careful work of a similar nature was also required whenever a customer ordered an exact copy of some antique piece for inclusion in his private collection. The mid and late nineteenth century in England was a period of outstanding eclectic activity in almost every subject, but none more so than in the field of English ceramics, both Roman, medieval, and post-medieval in date. Aided by such well-illustrated volumes as Marryatt's *Collections towards a History of Pottery* of 1850, Chaffer's *Marks and Monograms on Pottery and Porcelain* of 1863, Jewitt's formidable *Ceramic Art of Great Britain* of 1878, and Solon's *Art of the Old English Potter* of 1883, many English collectors were able to obtain precise reproductions of the wares they collected by having them made to their particular specification at a local pottery. Both the Harrises of Farnham and the Binghams of Castle Hedingham were particularly competent in this work, producing either Roman or medieval wares in quite a convincing manner whenever the occasion demanded. In many cases the potters were still using centuries-old sources of clay and glaze and were thus able to make detail-perfect reproductions, some of which have only recently been discovered within the national collections. It was not only English wares that were made in this way, for the growing habit of museum visiting was bringing the glories of European and Asian ceramics to the attention of the general public for the first time. Russian, German, Belgian and French wares, the latter including the detailed products of Palissy himself, were all copied for the collector's market. Even the wares of Troy and Mycenae, excavated by Schliemann from 1871 onwards and later exhibited in London, were copied in quantity. J. Phillips, the Devonshire historian, noted that 'a new direction was given to the sgraffito pottery of north Devon by Mr Fishley of Fremington, whose acquaintance I then made, and subsequently, on his application, had the pleasure of accompanying him through some of the best collections of pottery in London, which were likely to be useful to him, including Dr Schliemann's many pieces, of which he sketched, and very cleverly reproduced.' Similar work was also done at the same period by Mrs Fred Mitchell of the Belle Vue Pottery, Rye, no less than eighteen different shapes of her 'Trojan Ware' being made in faithful imitation of Schliemann's major ceramic exhibits.

Besides making copies of valuable antique pieces for individual collectors, a number of potters discovered the financial advantages of forging early wares, frequently completing them in an 'antique' style with seventeenth- or eighteenth-century dates. Fortunately modern scholarship can easily detect such wares, for the majority of their makers had only a rudimentary knowledge of early ceramic designs and materials. Should a late nineteenth-century forgery be discovered in a collection, however, it should not be discarded. Such pieces often reflect the potter's own feelings of what a good-quality antique earthenware pot should have been like, and they are usually of excellent workmanship. Of particular interest are the 'Old English' two-handled mugs made by C. H. Brannam of Barnstaple in the 1880s. One of these, presented to the North Devon Athenaeum in 1883 by the maker, is inscribed 'Words are easy/Like the wind/Faithful friends/Are hard to find/1766', while a further example, now in the Burton Art Gallery, Bideford, bears the inscription 'If ye can't lie aisy/Be as aisy/as ye/can/1821', thus proving that an early date is not sufficient evidence alone for an early pot.

The experience gained in copying different types of ware for the collector soon proved to be of the greatest possible advantage, for during the early 1880s a popular demand for aesthetically designed 'art wares' arose throughout the country. The Arts and Crafts Movement propagated by such powerful writers as John Ruskin and William Morris was advocating the creation of beauty through craftsmanship, so encouraging the foundation of a number of 'art pottery' studios where decorative wares of a supremely high aesthetic quality were produced by well-educated artist-potters. Like all works of art, the studio productions were expensive, being made in relatively small numbers. They took many hours of patient hand work to complete, and long periods of experimentation with such costly materials as metallic oxides, lustres

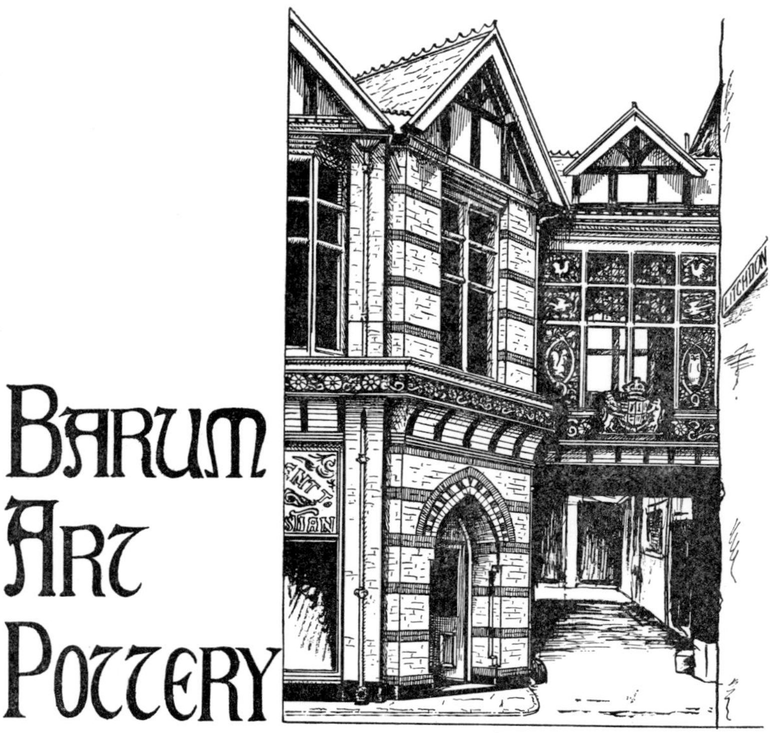


Fig 2 The entrance and showroom of C. H. Brannam's Pottery in Barnstaple

and frits were necessary to achieve the artist's high ideals. Obviously it was only the upper classes who could afford to buy the fashionable works of the De Morgan, Martin or Doulton studios, but the coarse earthenware potter was perfectly capable of supplying the average household with cheaper substitutes which, even if they lacked a certain degree of aesthetic finesse, were certainly well made technically. By the addition of the cheaper metallic oxides and the newly developed range of Wenger's colours he was able to evolve particularly rich polychrome decorations in the naturalistic, 'aesthetic', Japanese or medieval styles to compete in the lower reaches of the art pottery trade. Some potters, however, such as Absolom Harris of Farnham[6] or C. H. Brannam of Barnstaple, were able to build up quite a considerable reputation for their art products, sending regular supplies to Heal's, Liberty's and the Rural Industries Society in London, and also building extensive showrooms at their potteries to display their new series of ornamental wares.

In many ways the fashion for art pottery came at a very convenient time for the country potter, for most of his traditional markets were beginning to disappear, the craft slowly passing into its final phase of decline. Its success had always depended on the existence of large poorly paid communities who could not afford superior wares, but by the mid-nineteenth century the general standard of living was steadily rising, bringing with it increased prosperity and numerous changes in the average way of life. The advantages of the urban situation were being realised and accepted. Brewing, for example, was ceasing to be a domestic craft, as it was now much cheaper and easier to buy one's beer at one of the corner beer houses. Although half the beer made in England was home brewed in 1800, by 1850 the proportion was down to one-seventh, falling to one-fortieth in 1870[7], thus illustrating the decline in home brewing, and hence in the sale of brewing pots also. Home baking suffered a similar fate as new town bakeries were built, killing the demand for baking bowls and yeast pots. Other domestic operations were also ceasing to be practised in the towns about the same time. Butter was no longer being preserved by the stone in tall butter pots, hams and pork joints were not being home cured in large earthenware brine pots, and pilchards were not being salted down in the Cornish bussas in the same quantities as before. New materials were coming into increased use too, as enamelled metal, tinplate, galvanised iron and mould-blown glass replaced coarse earthenware as a medium for drinking vessels, bottles or storage containers.

In addition to this loss of trade the country potter had also to face a fresh spate of competition from the pottery factories of Staffordshire, which now began to compete with him in the production of cheap tablewares such as jugs, mugs, plates and teapots. By the diffusion of mass-production moulding and casting techniques throughout the factories it was now possible for them to offer the public good quality white wares at an economical figure for the first time. The wares they offered were bright, clean-looking and light in weight; their glazes were clear and glossy and their decoration, either transfer-printed or hand-painted, made them particularly attractive. Now the working classes were quite prepared to pay a little more for pottery of this superior type, for as their wages had risen by an estimated 30 per cent between the 1850s and 1880s,[8] it was at last within their reach. The effects of the competition from the factories had first been felt during the second quarter of the nineteenth century, but the growing demand for either horticultural wares or art wares had enabled most of the country potters to remain in production, even though a steady succession of closures had taken place from the 1860s onwards. When war broke out in 1914 it had a catastrophic effect on the craft, for it effectively removed the demand for most of the potter's financially worthwhile products, besides which both skilled men and their apprentices were conscripted into the armed forces. Many potteries were thus forced into permanent closure, but for those which survived a period of new prosperity ensued in the post-war years. Art wares, especially if brightly coloured, were more popular than ever before, while all forms of architectural ceramics came to be required in ever-increasing quantities as new housing schemes got under way. A few of the more successful potteries even went through a brief period of expansion in the early 1920s, often installing steam power and employing staffs of twenty or more in an attempt to convert their small family concerns into viable businesses; but within a few years the depression of the mid-twenties and thirties had set in, and men had to be laid off as customer after customer began to cancel his orders. Additional losses of trade were also experienced about this time because of the replacement of the horse and cart with the motorised delivery vehicle. Town-based grocers and bakers could now serve much greater areas than ever before, bringing the urban advantages of factory-prepared breads, preserved meats and dairy products into the rural areas and thus removing the need for home baking and preserving, for which considerable quantities of earthenware had been made. In 1939 war once more brought fuel rationing, the necessity of blackouts for the kilns, the loss of sufficient markets and, again, the conscription of the potters and their apprentices. These pressures, combined with the difficulties of the inter-war years, greatly accelerated the demise of the craft. Whereas there had been well over a hundred country potteries working in England in 1900, by 1945 there were less than a dozen, and the majority of these were operated by men who had been training during the prosperous years immediately before and after World War I, and who were now approaching middle age. During the early post-war years these potteries tried to raise the craft up to its former strength. The public were evidently interested in their products, for articles on them appeared in numerous country and county magazines, while a nation-wide throwing competition for professional earthenware potters became one of the most popular features of the Royal Show. The demand for horticultural wares such as plant pots and terrace jars was growing steadily, but before this demand could be met the potters had to have a sufficient number of trained craftsmen on their staffs. Men returning from war service, however, preferred easier occupations, and so the majority of the remaining country potters were forced to work on as one-man concerns, their potteries closing on their retirement. Thus the recent history of the country potteries has been one of slow and inevitable collapse. In 1945 Richard Bateson closed the last of the Burton-in-Lonsdale potteries, in 1955 Mesech Sims closed the last of the Verwood potteries, in 1964 Isaac Button closed the last Halifax pottery, while in 1970 Fishley Holland, last of the north Devon potters, died.

In England today there are only two working potteries[9] in which the traditional hand-techniques alone are practised. Both are family concerns, and both have had the extreme good fortune to find sons and grandsons to take over their management. If they can continue to work economically without the installation of pottery-making machinery the craft will continue, but if not, the skills, knowledge and experience of this thousand-year-old tradition will be lost entirely.

## *Note*

This chapter has been solely concerned with the wares of the country potter who dug his own clay, processed it himself, and who formed, glazed and fired it using the traditional materials and methods of his own particular region. A great number of new potteries have been opened in recent years by art-school-trained potters who use bought-in materials, and who work outside the traditions of their own region, and who are thus beyond the scope of the present volume.

*Notes for this chapter are on page 177*

## *Chapter Two*

# *Materials and Techniques*

It is advisable to study the materials and techniques of manufacture of a piece of country pottery in some detail, for these features alone are usually sufficient to enable its origins to be established with a fair degree of certainty. The colour and texture of the fabric, the method of decoration and the ways in which the glaze has been stained or dipped differ from one potting area to another. In some cases, where a particularly distinctive shape has been used or where certain stamps or other decorative features have been applied, it is even possible to attribute a piece to an individual potter. These instances are comparatively rare, but even quite plain pots can be attributed to their respective communities, such as Sussex, west Yorkshire or north Devon, solely by the appearance of their component materials.

## *Fabrics*

Perhaps the most difficult feature to identify is the unglazed fabric of which the pot is made, for although this changes with the geological area, the visual differences between one fired clay and another are usually very slight. Should the pot have a red fabric, for example, it could easily have been made anywhere from Kent to Northumberland, for the majority of English potting clays contain sufficient iron to burn to a full red colour in the kiln. The actual tone of the colour is of little help for identification, for this merely reflects the temperature to which the pot was fired, a bright orange-red resulting from a low firing of 600–700°C, while a dark red or purple would be produced at 1,050 or 1,100°C. Due to the crude stoking techniques and the lack of any accurate temperature recording devices, it was impossible for the potters to fire their kilns with any degree of scientific accuracy. There might easily be a 200° difference in temperature between the top and bottom of a kiln at any one time, and so the resultant wares were sure to emerge in a wide range of tonal finishes. The texture of most redware is similarly undistinguished, too, for the coarse and rather open fabrics usually exhibit the presence of varying degrees of sand or grit, together with minute bubble-like hollows which pierce the surface where impurities burnt off during the firing.

Some areas, however, have particularly distinctive colours and textures of fabric. Of these, the most easily recognisable are those of the north Devon potteries, which have a fine flesh-coloured fabric ranging from a pale terracotta to a pale buff in tone. This unusual colour is combined with a smooth, compact and bubble-free surface which feels rather chalky to the touch when clean and dry. In Cornwall, where a small number of wares were made from certain beds of local clay, the fabrics possess the unique feature of minute flakes of mica distributed evenly throughout their thickness. Although these particles are well under $\frac{1}{16}$ in across, they can easily be seen on the pink to mid-red unglazed surfaces, their glass-like crystals usually being soft enough to be scratched by a hard rub of the thumbnail.[1] The products of the Verwood kilns at the western edge of the New Forest also have a distinctive fabric, but this is of a dirty mid-buff colour with a coarse gritty texture which presents a relatively uneven and lumpy surface, frequently broken up into wide reticulations by a series of fine cracks which result from the potter's extremely crude firing techniques. A little to the east, at Farnham in Surrey, a particularly pure white clay was worked for the finer products of the potteries in Farnham, in the Blackwater valley, and also in Fareham in Hampshire. When fired, this fabric presented a very pale creamy-white surface rendered slightly rough by the projection of numerous particles of a rather darker grit. As the Farnham claypit was apparently in continuous use from the late medieval period up to the 1930s (with a brief closure from 1865 to 1885) it can be extremely difficult to distinguish between a genuine medieval piece and a reproduction made in the same manner some four hundred years later. Throughout the north and the midlands the majority of the potteries were built on the coal-measure series where a fine buff-coloured fireclay was readily available. Although this material usually contained large amounts of coarse grit which enabled it to be fired to extremely high temperatures, many potters employed it occasionally for making earthenwares, glazing it with their normal lead glazes.

Wherever the potters had the choice of two clays of different colours, usually a red and a white, they developed various techniques of mixing one coarsely with the other to make an ornamental marbled clay known variously as 'agate', 'grained' or 'snail-horn' ware. This was extremely popular in the late nineteenth-century potteries of Sussex, Lancashire, Yorkshire, Cumberland and Westmorland in particular.

## *Potting*

The processes of converting the raw clay into useful wares were surprisingly uniform throughout the country, for although the style of the individual tools varied from one area to another, the actual techniques of potting were almost identical. The most common method was, of course, throwing. The potter began this operation by banging a lump of plastic and well-kneaded clay down on to the rapidly rotating potter's wheel. Then, lubricating his hands with water, he firmly squeezed the clay until it become perfectly centred on the wheel-head, this being essential if worthwhile pots were to be produced. The mass of clay was then hollowed to form a tall cylinder which could be either enlarged or constricted by the potter to make any particular shape he required. A taut wire was then pulled horizontally across the wheel-head, slicing the pot free so that it could be transported to a rack of open shelves to dry before being fired. In most parts of the country the operations of throwing were all carried out by hand, this method alone being responsible for the flowing lines and slightly rippled surfaces which enliven most country-made pots. Some nineteenth-century potters, however, preferred to use sharply defined templates or 'ribs' in their throwing, pressing these wooden or sheet-metal silhouettes against the outer surfaces of their pots as they revolved, thus bringing them to a precise and uniform finish. Pottery made in this way always possesses a rather harsh machine-made character, its sharp, over-neat mouldings obviously being unnatural to a wheel-made piece. A few potteries, such as the Woodman House Pottery, near Halifax, and the Farnham Pottery in Surrey,

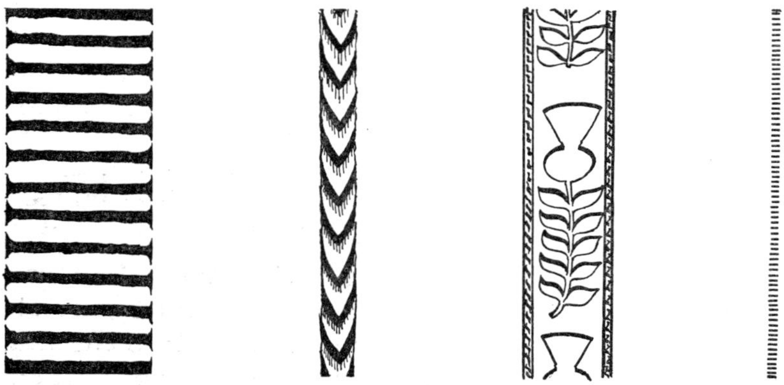

Fig 3 Rouletted decorations drawn from (left to right) Farnham Pottery, Surrey; Woodman House Pottery, Halifax; a jar at Hartlebury Castle, Worcestershire; and a Sussex flask in the Greg Collection at Manchester (no. 1947.602)

used a roulette to impress a decorative strip round their pots as they revolved on the wheel. When this method was practised in a restrained manner it could be particularly effective, as is demonstrated by a huge jar at Hartlebury Castle in Worcestershire, for example. Besides these rather obvious features, a number of more subtle clues to a pot's origins may be noted by careful examination.

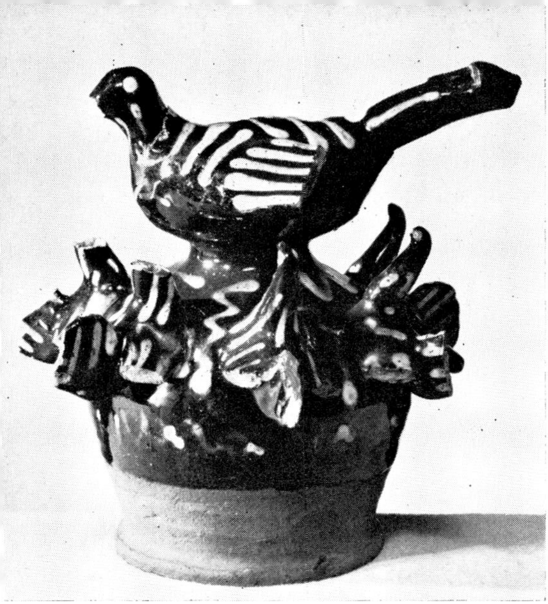

*Page 35* Money boxes made (*left*) at Gorsty Hill, Worcestershire and (*below*) at Burton-in-Lonsdale, Yorkshire (see notes on page 181)

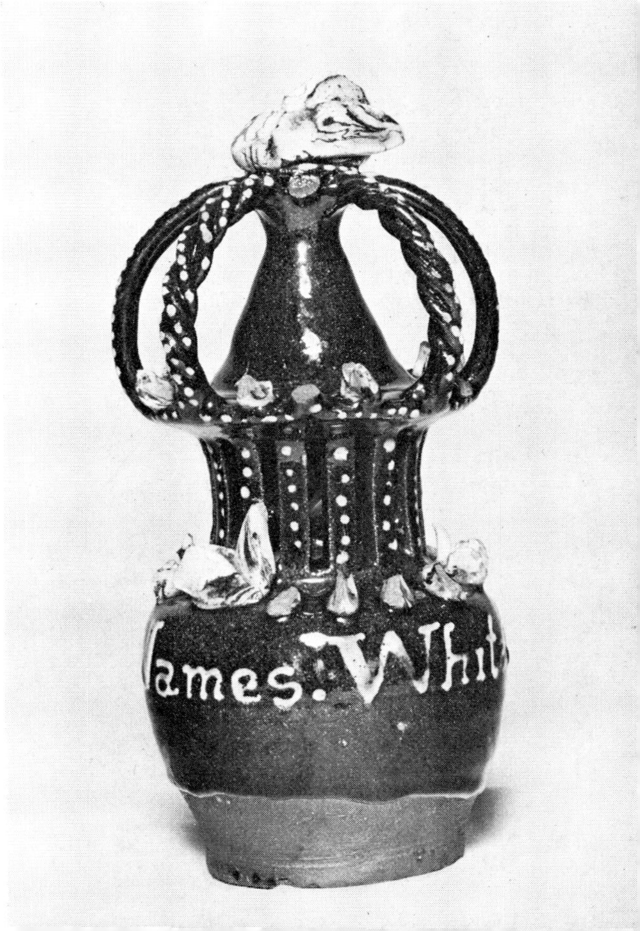

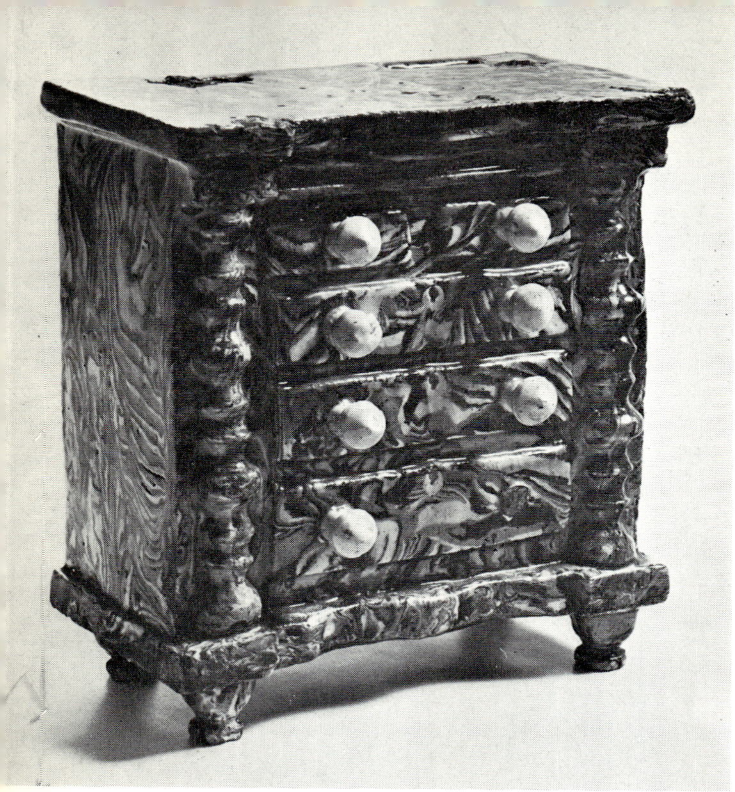

*Page 36* Money boxes made (*above*) in Halifax in 1846 and (*right*) by William Freemantle Harris of Farnham, *c*.1890 (see notes on page 182)

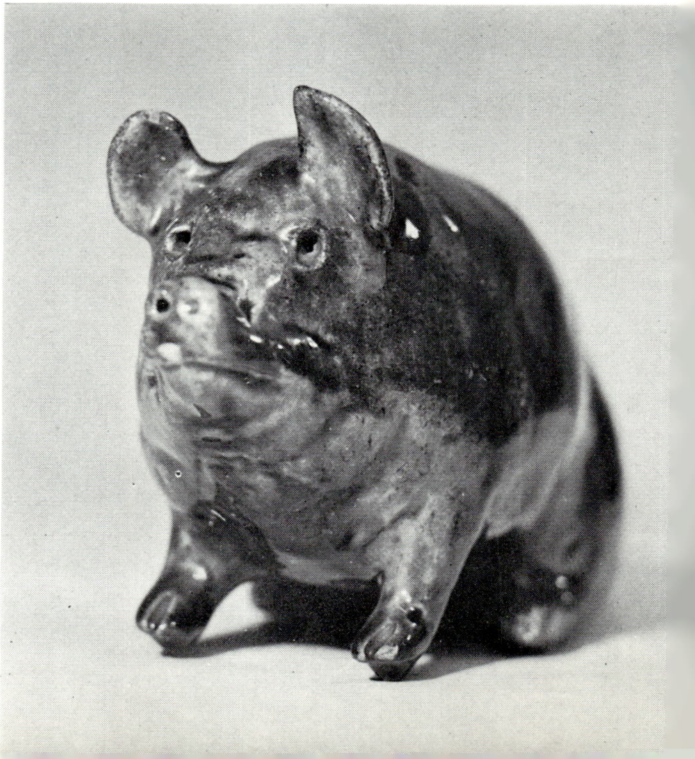

When comparing one pot with another from a known source, for example, it is always wise to check that both pieces were made by a potter who was either left or right handed, as a left-handed potter would never have made a right-handed pot, and vice versa. To check on the direction of throwing, examine carefully the inner and outer surfaces of the pot where (unless the pot has a particularly sound and opaque glaze) you will find that either the 'grain' of the fabric or the crackle of the glaze follows a spiral course. If this grain runs from the top left to bottom right of the outer surface of the pot then it must have been made by a right-handed potter, the plastic clay being pulled up into a cylinder on the wheel by a man working on its right-hand side. Should the grain run from bottom left to top right, however, then the pot can have been made only by a left-handed potter. If the grain is visible only on the inner surfaces, then the directions are reversed, of course, top left to bottom right for left-handed, and bottom left to top right for right-handed.

A study of the underside of any thrown pot can also provide interesting comparative evidence for linking one group of vessels with another, for many potters developed a particular method of slicing their pots from the wheel-head. Most used a single length of wire, holding it taut across the wheel and slicing off the pot with a steady straight pull. This left the bottom of the pot quite smooth, but any coarse particles in the clay were pulled along by the wire to leave a number of shallow scratches on the surface behind them (fig 4A). Other potters however, such as Harry Thorburn of Penrith, preferred to loop their wires round the pot's base, gradually constricting the loop until the pot was free. This technique resulted in a series of irregular leaf-shaped loops being cut across the base as the wire slowly forced its way through the uniform clay (fig 4B). Where the potter preferred to use a twisted double wire instead of the more normal single variety, the surface was left in a series of regular shallow flutes, each representing a twist along the length of wire (fig 4C). This particular method is uncommon, being rarely seen except on mid-eighteenth-century or earlier wares. When other bases are examined in detail they will often present smooth spiral patterns in very low relief (fig 4D) in which case

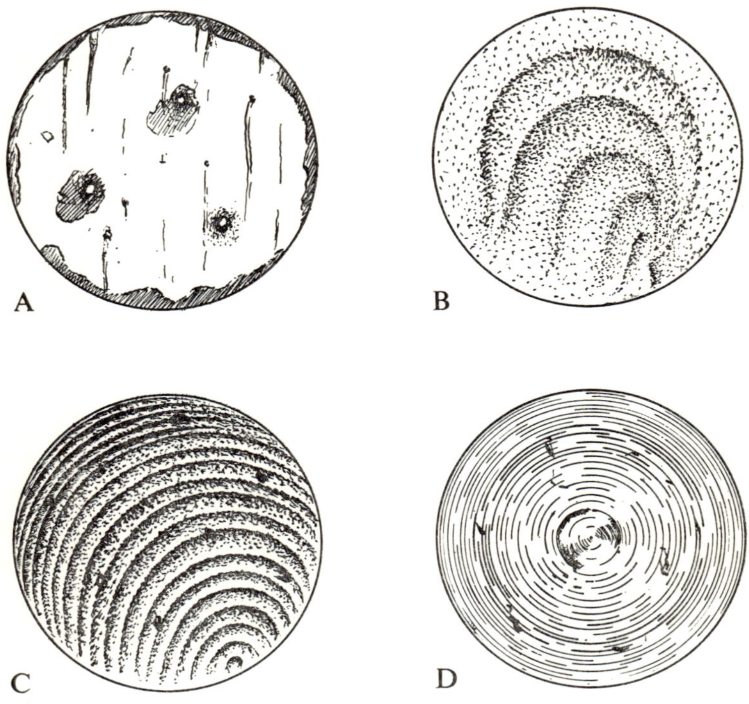

Fig 4 Base scars showing the results of (A) slicing with a straight pull of a single wire; (B) slicing with an encircling wire; (C) slicing with an encircling multi-strand wire; and (D) turning off surplus clay on the potter's wheel. Base A also shows the scars caused by glaze sticking the pot to its three-legged support during the firing

they must have been 'turned' by being carefully mounted concentrically on the wheel in an inverted position, and having their rough under-surfaces neatly scraped off by a sharp chisel-edged tool as they slowly revolved. This technique was particularly time-consuming, and so was normally reserved for such high-quality pieces as inlaid Sussex jars, or fine northern agate-wares.

Although the vast majority of the potter's produce was thrown on the wheel, large numbers of vessels were also made by pressing slabs of clay into or round specially prepared moulds of earthenware or plaster. From the mid-seventeenth century at least plates were being rapidly made by rolling out thin sheets of clay which were then patted and pressed into shape over mushroom-shaped moulds of unglazed earthenware. Wares formed in this manner are quite easy to identify, for their walls are always of a uniform thickness throughout; they have no wire-cuts or turning marks on their bases, and they are often square or rectangular in plan. Unlike thrown wares, they lack any form of roll or moulding round their edges, for these are either knife cut and carefully smoothed to a regular section, or else they are impressed with a coarsely-ridged roulette to give a neatly scalloped rim. Larger wares, such as late nineteenth-century troughs and garden urns, were also press-moulded from unglazed earthenware or plaster of Paris moulds. For these three-dimensional pieces, which often boasted ornate decorative motifs in high relief, the potter was forced to make the pot in sections. To do this he had to beat thick slabs of clay into each component part of his sectional mould, finally uniting one cast clay detail with another to make up the complete article. Often a skilfully moulded vessel may pass as a thrown piece, but usually a thorough examination will reveal the moulding scars within the detailing, or slight variations in the thickness of the walls round the pot's circumference, both features being entirely absent from the wheel-made examples.

Some of the most interesting methods of potting required the minimum of tools and equipment, the potter's hands and feet alone, with the possible exception of a knife or rolling pin, being used to shape the clay. These methods, classified by the general term of forming, may be broadly divided into two sections: oven-building and slab-building. Oven-building became an extremely sophisticated craft skill in many west country potteries from the early seventeenth century at least, vast domed ovens being made up to 3ft in height from the gravel-tempered clays of Devon and Cornwall.[2] Slab-building, meanwhile, was mainly a north-country technique, and consisted of building up such items as miniature cradles, rocking chairs, chests of drawers or knife-trays from slabs of clay rolled out to about $\frac{1}{4}$in in thickness, these being carefully cut out and then stuck together with a thick slip.

## *Decorating*

The methods of decorating country pottery were always extremely simple, for the average potter lacked the time and capital necessary to install complicated decorating equipment. This does not mean that the results he achieved were necessarily of a poor quality, for aesthetic appeal and technical excellence are certainly not synonymous. His finer products were made to the highest standards attainable with such simple tools as goose quills, cow's horns, a home-made stylus of wood, bone or metal or old printer's type. Using these in a completely unrestricted manner, completely free from the inhibitions of contemporary aesthetic thought and governed only by his regional tradition, he was able to produce extremely refined wares of superb quality. This applies mainly to those wares made between the seventeenth and mid-nineteenth centuries, for, in common with many other traditional art forms they tend to degenerate rapidly when a community becomes industrialised.

Of all the decorative techniques the simplest and earliest was slip-dipping, in which a pot with a red fabric was immersed in a tub of white slip. This was practised in most of the western counties from the early sixteenth century, some examples, such as the jugs in the County Museum, Truro, having been dipped as far as their spouts and fronts only, thus giving the pots broad white bibs to emphasise their forms. Other west-country examples, however, were completely immersed in the slip to give them an overall white colour, portions of which could be scratched away when dry to reveal the red fabric beneath.

This technique, now known by the Italian term *sgraffito*, developed slowly from the mid-sixteenth century, being chiefly practised in Donyatt in Somerset and in the north Devon potteries of Barnstaple and Bideford from this time up to the opening decades of the present century. It is sometimes difficult to determine at which of the above potteries a piece of sgraffito ware was made, for there are a number of similarities between them, and it has recently been proved that a potter and his family moved from Bideford to Donyatt in 1691.[3] Certain differences do exist, however. The Donyatt sgraffito wares tend to retain a white slip background to all their designs, the various scroll, rosette, tulip or cockerel motifs being executed in free curvilinear line-work alone. In addition, these wares usually contain patches of a green stain in their glaze (this being the result of cuprous impurities), but examples quite free from this characteristic are known. The north Devon wares, meanwhile, never exhibit green stains in their glazes, and frequently have the background portions of their designs scraped away to leave their white motifs standing out in slight relief above the basic red-brown fabric. A further group of extremely competent sgraffito wares was made in the Staffordshire potteries during the early to mid-eighteenth century. They normally have a very dark red slip over a pale buff-coloured fabric and are decorated with the boisterous figures of deer, lions or foliage in a direct linear style. The more refined pieces often have their fabric and slip colours reversed, the decoration in these cases being in the form of precisely cut chequers or turned bands. Frequently the better-quality pieces also bear rather large plain bands or rectangles of white slip in which either floral motifs or the date may be inscribed, the figures of the latter always having a characteristic bordering of dots which appears to be unique to this particular region and period.

In most other areas the sgraffito technique was only rarely used until the demand for decorative 'art' wares arose in the late nineteenth century, when it enjoyed great popularity. Many potters found that their art-conscious customers wished to design their own pieces of pottery, even though they entirely lacked the necessary skill and experience. To cater for this market the potters made and slipped 'artistic' shapes which were then sold in a raw state to the would-be potters, who decorated them as they wished. The pots were then returned to the pottery to be glazed and fired free of charge, as these services were included in the initial purchase price. There are few things quite so brittle as a dry raw pot, and only a small percentage of those wares sold can have survived the journeys to and from the customer's home, but this was of little consequence to the potter, for he made his profits entirely on the first payment. The wares made in this way vary tremendously in quality. A few pieces, such as those executed by Miss Daysh and Miss Hall of Farnham, are outstanding examples of period taste, as the plates and vases in the Allen Bequest at Alton prove, but others, to be found in every conceivable style and form, display the dullest and most incompetently executed designs imaginable. Perhaps the latest sgraffito wares to be commercially produced in England were the scent bottles, ash trays, mugs, cream jugs and the like made for the tourist trade of the south-western resorts. During the first half of the twentieth century such potteries as Brannam's of Barnstaple and the Aller Vale Pottery, Torquay, produced large numbers of these wares. They all have a dark red fabric coated with a white slip over which were brushed coloured slip illustrations of yachts, windmills or flowers, together with sgraffito inscriptions such as 'Dinna scale the cream', 'Real Devon Violets' or even 'Here's your Country's love to you, 1899–1900, God Bless You Tommy Atkins, South Africa', an Aller Vale speciality.

Sgraffito was not the only technique in which a dipped pot might be decorated, however, as a number of potters discovered in the mid-nineteenth century. If a number of thin and flexible motifs such as leaves or cut paper shapes were first smoothed down on to the half-dry surface of the ware and the whole pot was then dipped into a slip of a contrasting colour, they could then be carefully peeled off once the slip was almost dry to reveal the original fabric beneath. This 'resist' technique was used by surprisingly few potters, considering that it required so little effort yet gave quite attractive results. Some good examples are to be seen in the Bideford Library Museum, where one of George Fishley's pitchers bears a band of leaf-resist patterns round its neck, while a further jug there shows bushes of resist leaves sprouting from a number of scrolled sgraffito pots.

A further decorative technique which was often employed on dipped pots was combing, in which a blunt-toothed comb of wood, leather or metal was run through the moist slip coating to expose the underlying fabric. Although the potters of Donyatt in Somerset had been using this technique ever since the mid-seventeenth century, it too was developed to an outstanding degree by the Fishleys of Fremington in the mid- to late nineteenth century, the comb being replaced here by a specially constructed tool made from four whalebone prongs tipped with the teats from babies' bottles. Most later Fishley examples, such as those in the Victoria and Albert Museum in London have the flesh-coloured Fremington fabric covered in a beautifully combed white slip beneath a rich green glaze.

Besides being used as an over-all dip, slip could also be piped on to the ware through a fine quill, this extremely popular technique being known as slip-trailing. Although it was introduced into England from the continent only in the late sixteenth and early seventeenth centuries, this method became one of the most widely used, each potting region having its own particular designs and methods of application. In Westmorland, for example, the potters used a very thin slip which they trailed on to the ware through an $\frac{1}{8}$in-diameter goose quill mounted in the tip of a curved cow horn which acted as a reservoir.[4] With this tool the slip had to be applied with the utmost degree of speed and confidence, for the slightest halt would have resulted in the ware being flooded with surplus slip and consequently ruined. Twentieth-century Westmorland slip-trailing therefore has the quality of being extremely free in its handling, lines of uniform thickness zig-zagging confidently down the sides of tall pots without the slightest indication of any hesitation whatsoever. This rapid work was possible only with a fast-running supply of watery

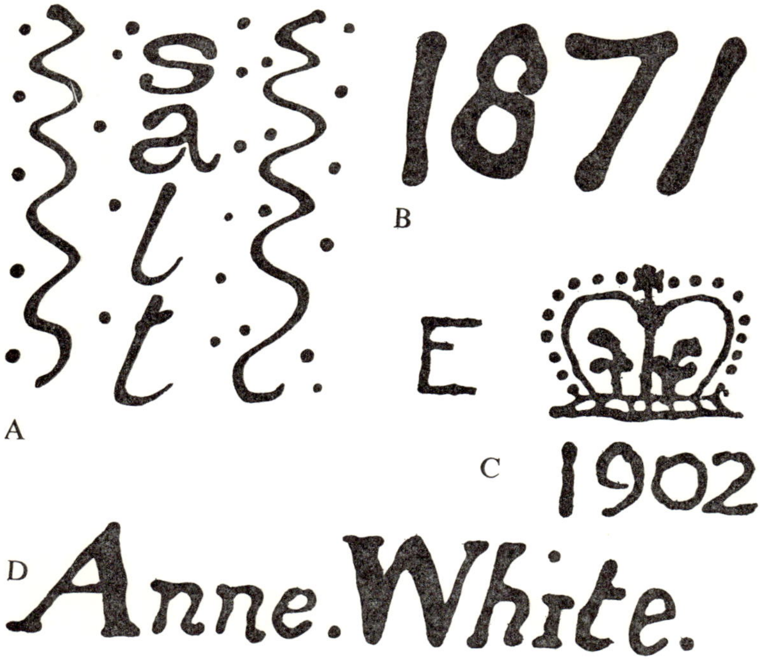


Fig 5 Slip-trailing styles from (A) Weatheriggs Pottery, Westmorland, (B) Halifax, Yorkshire, (C) Fremington Pottery, Devon, and (D) Burton-in-Lonsdale, Yorkshire

slip, and so the actual thickness of the slip coating is often very thin indeed, sometimes being barely perceptible under a normal coating of glaze. In Devon, where the same goose-quill and cow-horn trailer was used with a much thicker slip,[5] the trailing has a completely different character, for each line was slowly pulled out into place over the surface of the ware, the resultant lines being uneven in width and rather precise and angular in character. The consistency of the slip also caused it to stand up to a $\frac{1}{16}$in proud of the surface, even after it had been finally glazed and fired.

A rather different form of slip-trailer was used at the north-west Yorkshire pottery of Burton-in-Lonsdale.[6] Here the trailer was in the form of a $\frac{1}{4}$ pint bottle with a small hole near its base into which a quill could be inserted horizontally. In use, the bottle was filled with a fairly thick slip which was allowed to trickle out on to the ware, the lips being placed over the bottle's mouth to blow out more slip whenever necessary. In character the Burton-in-Lonsdale trailing is extremely competent and precise. On most of the wares, for example, the potter threw a narrow groove into the pot where any lettering was to be done, thus ensuring that it maintained a perfectly level course. Trailing then proceeded, every capital letter having the broad down-stroke, narrow up-stroke and fine serifs of a Roman-style printer's typeface, while the lower-case characters were trailed in clear and uniform line-work with full stops separating each word.

In Halifax, meanwhile, the potters used an extremely crude trailing device made from the bowl of an old clay pipe, the bowl itself acting as a reservoir for the slip, and a goose quill fitted over the broken stem as a nozzle. Holding the trailer either like a pen, or else in his clenched fist with his thumb over the top of the bowl and the quill protruding between his first and second fingers, the potter allowed the slip to ooze out on to the half-dry ware. Working with such a small volume of slip it was impossible to trail lines of any length, and so the use of relatively small slip patterns became one of the features of Halifax pottery.

Elsewhere in England it is almost impossible to determine how the slip-trailed line-work was executed, for no accurate records were made before the older potteries ceased production. From a close examination of the patterns on a number of surviving pieces, however, it is possible to determine where a piece originated from with a fair degree of accuracy, as will be shown in the following chapters.

Although slip was certainly the most popular decorative medium to be used in the country potteries over the last 250 years, it was by no means the only one, as the potters used every technique available to them to render their wares as attractive and saleable as possible. Their lack of capital prohibited their using such high-grade techniques as enamel painting, gilding or transfer printing, but by the skilful use of their basic clays and a few simple tools they were able to produce wares possessing a lively air of robust vitality. This quality is perhaps best seen where the potters applied their decoration in solid clay of different colours, building up their basic pottery shapes with scrolls or rolled clay, pinched-out knots or leaves or even free-standing figures of birds, animals or men. Work of this type had been extensively produced during the high medieval period, but from the early fifteenth century at least it had gradually lost its popularity, being continued only in the reduced greenware and Cistercian ware potteries in the north, and perhaps also in the dark-glaze potteries of south Wiltshire. From the mid-seventeenth century, a number of potteries at Wrotham in Kent, at Donyatt in Somerset and in the Stoke-on-Trent district of Staffordshire began to enrich the handles and mouldings of their wares with pellets, twisted bands and scrolls of clay, these being executed in a variety of colours wherever possible. Even though this form of decoration was quite effective the technique was still in its infancy, and it was not until the setting up of the urban potteries from the mid-eighteenth century onwards that any notable advances were made.

As the urban pottery trade expanded the potters discovered an increased demand for some of their ornamental wares, particularly those required for ceremonial occasions. To meet this demand three groups of potters in particular developed their own characteristic styles of decoration. The earliest of these worked in Staffordshire during the mid-eighteenth century, its work including money boxes, cradles etc, bearing beautifully modelled birds or figures. The outstanding example of this type, undoubtedly influenced by contemporary lead-glazed Aaron Wood figurines, is a cradle now in the Robert Hall Warren Collection at the Ashmolean Museum, Oxford. This has a white clay fiddler sitting astride its canopy, together with bewigged heads at each corner in place of the more usual plain knobs.

The second important group was made up of members of the Fishley family of the Fremington Pottery, situated between Barnstaple and Bideford on the north Devon coast. Their earlier work probably drew from the tradition of applied decoration founded at Donyatt in Somerset in the seventeenth century, but each generation of the family contributed a number of new forms and features. The earliest of these was George Fishley (1771–1865), probably the most important single earthenware potter of the nineteenth century, whose work includes large numbers of watch-pockets, animal groups, portrait figures, busts and so on, each being modelled in the liveliest of manners in a completely free and uninhibited style. He was one of the few English coarseware potters able to produce well-executed free-standing figures of men, women or animals entirely from his own experience, backed up by his strong north Devon potting tradition. Later potters certainly produced more polished and ambitious works, but almost without exception these were carried out in vain attempts to ape the antique, showing only the ability to copy, rather than the originality to pioneer an entirely fresh concept of decoration within the craft. George Fishley's two sons, Edmund (d. 1861) and Robert, also produced first-rate examples of applied decoration, the works of the former being particularly well executed, including such fine pieces as the Bideford wassail cup with its eight mural figures and fiddler terminal. Edmund's son, Edwin Beer Fishley (d. 1911), was the last of this family to make wares of such quality at Fremington, but as he was influenced by a number of local gentlemen who wished to 'improve' the artistic quality of his designs, much of his later work was based on Mycenaean, Etruscan, Staffordshire or Wrotham examples. The standard of workmanship displayed in these copies is such that the unwary collector may purchase a piece believing it to be genuinely early, but despite their quality they look rather lifeless against the full-blooded works of his father and grandfather.

The third group of potters to develop applied decoration to a high standard were the Kitsons of Ainley Top and Woodman House potteries near Halifax, Yorkshire. Here the majority of the modelling was carried out by Edward Kitson between 1836 and 1868, although even quite young members of the family, such as his daughter Elizabeth, occasionally made well-decorated pieces. Most of the applied decoration executed here was used to embellish such items as cradles, money boxes or even salt kits. One of the latter, decorated with three-dimensional birds and a dog, may be seen on page 107. Elsewhere applied decoration was used to only a limited degree by the country potters who worked within their local traditions, but as art wares became more and more popular in the mid-nineteenth century an increasing number of potters began to apply decorative clay motifs to their wares to render them more saleable.

Often the details applied to the pots were freely modelled by hand, but this could be an arduous and time-consuming operation when ornamental wares were being produced in fairly large numbers. A solution was found, however, in the use of small sprig-moulds which the potter could make for himself either from plaster of Paris or from unglazed clay. These were in the form of small blocks of a mould material into which were cut the negative forms of the leaves or figures which the potter wished to reproduce. In use, the potter pressed a small quantity of soft clay into the mould, scraping off any surplus with a straight-edge before carefully removing his 'sprig' or moulded detail, which could then be stuck to the surface of the ware with the aid of a little slip. At some potteries, such as that at Soil Hill, Halifax, the moulds were used in a rather different manner. Here the clay was first pressed into the mould, which, complete with its clay filling, was then pressed on to the surface of the pot itself, so sticking the sprigged detail down in position without its having to be removed separately from the mould, and thus saving much time and effort. At the same pottery some difficulty was experienced in firing wares with decoration applied in different clays. If a white sprig was fired on a red pot it tended to contract at a different rate when cooling, and so pulled itself away from the pot's surface. To remedy this a roll of red clay was often stuck round each applied detail, thus forming a frame in which it could contract without peeling off.

Throughout the history of hand-made pottery one of the simplest decorative techniques has consisted of incising or stamping designs into the surface of the wares, this being much simpler and quicker than sticking on additional clay details. With a pointed stick it was quite easy to scratch a name, date or pattern into the unfired clay but, as many potters began to realise from the mid to late eighteenth century, this rather crude technique was capable of being developed to produce quite fine and delicate results. At potteries in Nottingham and Sussex in particular it became the practice to cut linear designs into the surface of the leather-hard pottery, these incisions then being filled with a clay of a contrasting colour to produce particularly sharp and well-defined patterns once the surfaces had been cleaned off. During the early nineteenth century this technique spread to other urban potteries in various parts of the country, but the Sussex potters still produced the most competently executed inlaid decoration. One of the most characteristic features of their wares is the use of printer's type to form the impression to be inlaid, so enabling the potter to achieve the clarity and precision of printed lettering for running inscriptions round his tea caddies, flasks or harvest bottles.

In addition to these purely ceramic methods of decoration the use of oil paints was often resorted to, as this gave a much wider range of colours than was possible by the use of clays and slips alone. Occasionally a basic coating of oil-bound Prussian blue waggon paint would be brushed over a pot's surface to render it a little brighter or (in the case of Dorset pills from Verwood)[7] a little more waterproof, but more frequently the painting would take the form of fine polychrome illustrations of popular subjects. A magnificent example of this technique is to be seen at Shibden Hall, Halifax, where a large posset pot from the nearby Bate Hayne pottery bears a freely painted lion and unicorn, together with the initials 'C.I.A.1737' (see page 18). Unfortunately many collectors and curators consider that such over-glaze painting detracts from the value of a pot, and so strip it down to the basic glaze; this is an ignorant and ill-informed procedure which cannot be sufficiently condemned.

## *Glazes*

In common with clay fabrics, the final layer of glaze which covers most country pottery is extremely difficult to relate to any particular potter or pottery, for very similar materials were used by the members of each potting community. By dipping or brushing on to the wares a wet mixture of either red lead, litharge (lead monoxide) or galena (lead sulphide) with either sand or clay, and later firing them to about 1,000° C in the kiln, the potters were able to produce a variety of shining and waterproof glazes. Their colours and textures depended greatly on the types of clay to which they were applied, on the temperature to which they were fired, on the type of fuel used and also on the presence of any metallic oxides which might occur either accidentally or deliberately in their constituent materials. Much of the pottery made in the last 250 years came from the coal-measure regions of the north and midlands, in which the potteries of Whitehaven, Weatheriggs, Burton-in-Lonsdale, Halifax, Cliviger and north Staffordshire in particular were situated. Here the red clay appeared in a variety of brown tones beneath its yellow-tinted transparent glaze, a hazel colour resulting from a fairly low temperature firing of about 950–1,000°C, while rich gravy-browns and near-blacks were achieved at about 1,050–1,100° C. A further characteristic of these wares was the occurrence of thousands of minute white to yellow particles resting on the surface of the pot beneath the glaze. Although these are only about $\frac{1}{64}$in or less in length and width they are quite distinctive, enabling these northern redwares to be distinguished from those of the southern potteries with comparative ease. In Sussex, for example, where red-firing clay was also glazed to a range of warm brown tones, there are none of these small particles, but instead the glaze is speckled with numerous stains of a dark brown to metallic black colour resulting from the tiny iron impurities to be found in the Wealden clays. Further to the west, at Verwood on the perimeter of the New Forest, the potters used a straw-coloured lead glaze over their buff fabric to give their wares a golden yellow to pale orange finish. Here the only impurities were likely to be small mounds of pale-yellow sulphur about $\frac{1}{32}$in or less in diameter, these being remains of the raw glaze mixture which had failed to burn out during the firing. This particular phenomenon, known as sulphuration, may be seen on pottery from other areas too, often making a pot look as if it had been spattered with scrambled egg; it appears quite regularly on Verwood wares, though it is rarely seen elsewhere. In Cornwall and north Devon, where furze (gorse) was often used as the sole fuel, the colours of the glazes varied greatly with the change of season. In the spring, for example, when the freshly cut furze was rich in sap, the pots emerged from the kiln a dark green to yellow colour, often being mottled with a few pale orange patches and dark dots where particles of burning furze had settled on their glazes. The pots fired in June usually presented a fairly even khaki colour, while those fired from August onwards were of a particularly rich red-brown, the dryness of the fuel affecting the oxygen content of the kiln and hence causing these colour variations which appear to be unique to areas using this particular fuel.[8] As in the coal-measure regions these wares often contain minute pale yellow particles beneath their glazes, but because of the flesh colour of their fabrics and the colour variations described above, it is usually quite easy to differentiate between the wares of one region and the other.

Besides glazing their wares with plain lead glazes many potters also added metallic oxides to their basic mixtures to produce different colours. Perhaps the most commonly used oxide was that of iron, which stained the glaze to a dark brown or metallic black colour, depending on the percentage added. Stained iron glazes were common in the potteries of Essex, Staffordshire, Derbyshire and Yorkshire in particular from the mid-seventeenth century at least, and they continued to be widely used up to a few decades ago. Manganese could also be added to the glaze in oxide form, this giving a slightly speckled purple-brown colour as opposed to the red-browns produced by iron. This too was used in seventeenth-century Staffordshire and Derbyshire, particularly for finely thrown ale pots. It also saw service in the potteries of south Wiltshire, where it was used to glaze ornate jugs and posset pots; in the Cadborough Pottery, Rye, where it gave a speckled effect to art wares; and in the Fremington Pottery, where the Fishley family occasionally used it to darken some of their clay figures. Green glazes, meanwhile, were made by the addition of a copper oxide, the technique being identical to that used to produce the Tudor Greenwares of sixteenth- and seventeenth-century Surrey. From the 1860s, however, green glazes became popular once more, being used by the potters of the southern counties for their ornamental wares rather than for their everyday products.

When a coating of raw glaze had been applied the ware had then to be fired to around 1,000°C to bring it to maturity. During the sixteenth and seventeenth centuries a number of intricate techniques had been evolved to prevent the various pots from fusing inseparably together in the intense heat of the kiln, but by the mid-eighteenth century these had been largely superseded thanks to improvements in kiln design. Perhaps the most important of these improvements was the introduction of series of shelves or cupboards of stone or fireclay round the interior walls of the kiln, on which the glazed wares might be stacked. If the potter omitted to apply the glaze mixture to the lower inch or two of each pot he could simply stand them on the shelves and begin his firing, for there was no risk of their adhering irretrievably to the kiln. If the pot was a fine piece, however, and required an all-over

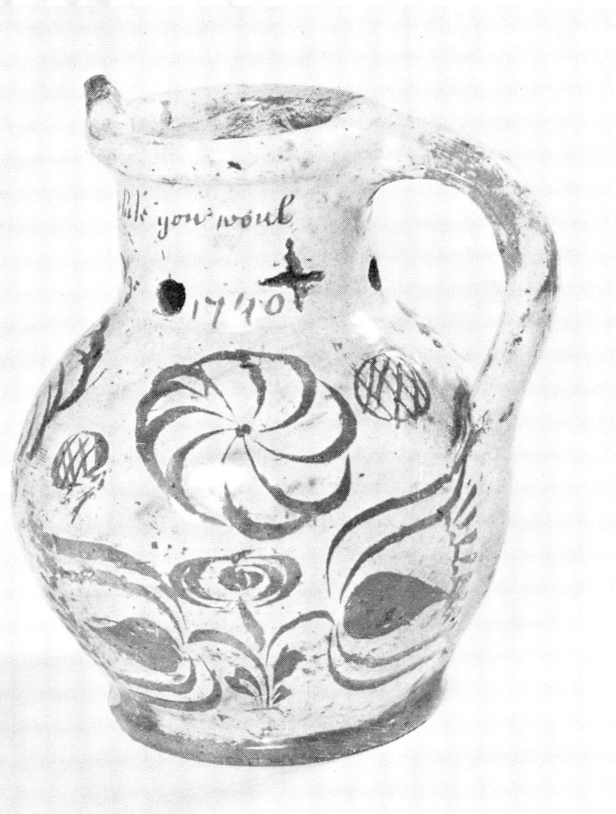


*Page 53* A puzzle jug of 1740 (*left*) and a set of 'Jolly Boys' of the late eighteenth century (*below*) both made at the Donyatt potteries (see notes on page 182)

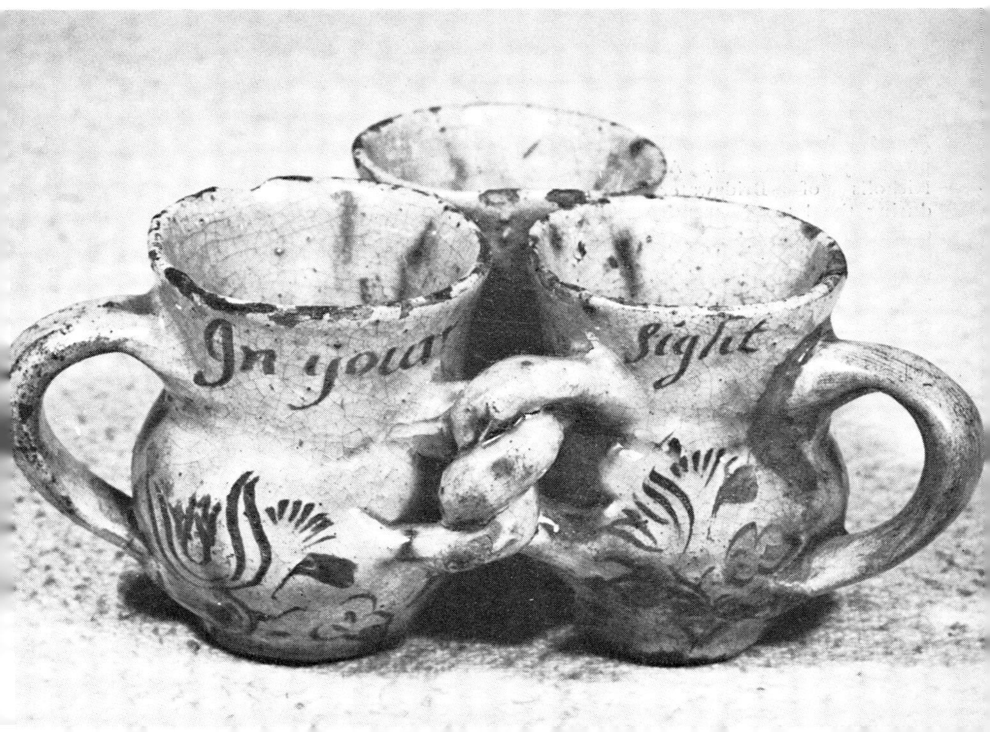

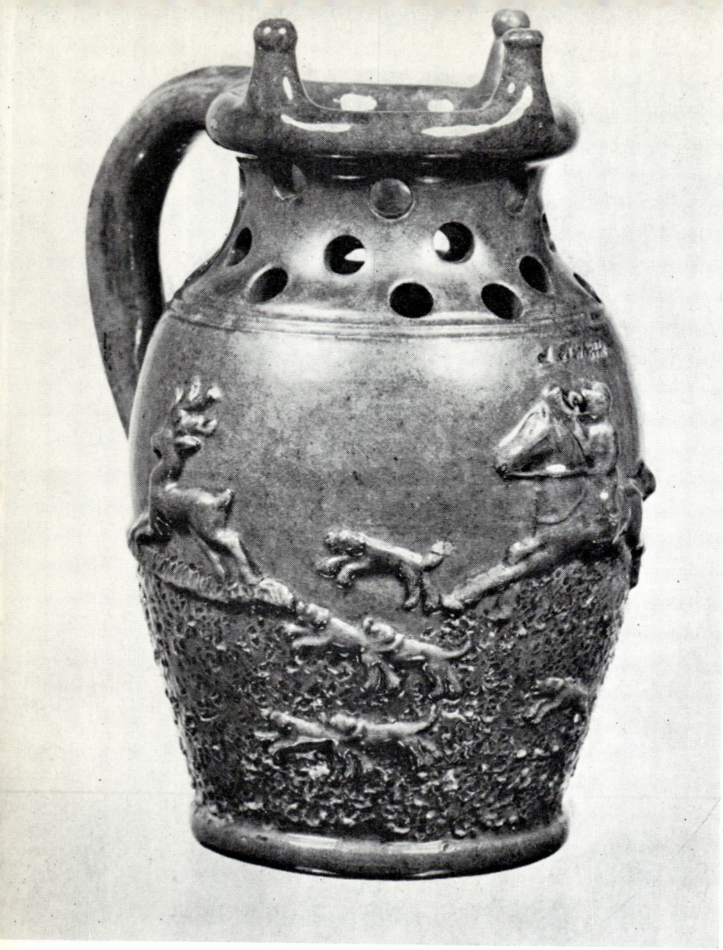

*Page 54* A sprig-moulded puzzle jug made by A. Nicholls of Bridgwater during the late nineteenth century (*above*) and a frog mug fired in the last kiln-load of the Howcans Pottery, Halifax in 1889 (*right*) (see notes on page 182)

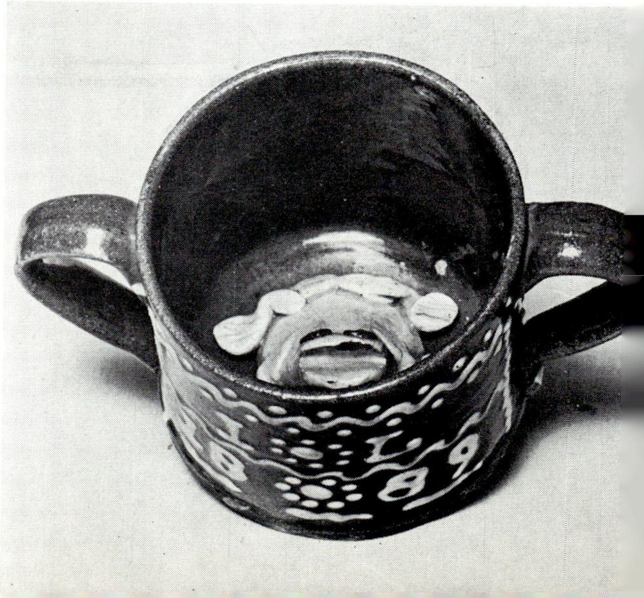

glaze, some means of propping had to be provided. In most potteries this need was met by the adoption of three-legged 'cockspurs' or tripod supports, which used three spikes of clay to raise each pot clear of the shelves. When the kiln had been fired and the wares had been carried out it was quite a simple matter to chip away the cockspurs to leave three minimal scars beneath the otherwise perfectly glazed pot (see fig 4A on page 38).

*Notes for this chapter are on pages 177–8*

## *Chapter Three*

# *Money Boxes*

Although a number of small earthenware money boxes had been made during the medieval period, this particular type of pot did not become really popular in England until the late sixteenth century, when large quantities began to be made for the London market. Most of the money boxes made at this time were about the size and shape of a large onion, having a small flat base, a bulbous body pierced by a vertical coin slot and a conical neck terminating in a round knob finial. Presumably this knob was quite an important feature, as it enabled the pot to be hung up. Higins, in his 1585 translation of *Junius Nomenclature*, mentioned 'a mony box mad of potters clay, wherein boyes put their money to keepe, such as they hang in shops etc towards Christmas (p 249). These money boxes were the original Christmas boxes used by the apprentices to collect their traditional gifts on the day after Christmas, which is still known as Boxing Day for this very reason. Having collected his gifts, the careful apprentice could use his knife to ease each coin in turn from the narrow slot, but the usual course was to break the pot open immediately, damaging it beyond repair in the process. When H. Browne was writing his *Mass of the Microcosme* in 1642, for example, he likened the covetous person to 'the Christmas earthen boxes of apprentices, apt to take in money, but he restores none till he be broken, like a potter's vessell, into many shares'. Many broken examples of these sixteenth- and seventeenth-century money boxes have been recovered from excavations carried out within the London area. Almost without exception they have been made in a hard fine-textured white or off-white fabric covered with a glossy vivid green glaze, often enlivened with a slightly iridescent finish. These are the characteristic materials of the Tudor Greenwares of Surrey origin, and it is interesting to note that identical money boxes have been discovered recently on the contemporary pottery-kiln sites of Ash and Farnborough Hill in West Surrey, thus proving their origins almost conclusively.[1]

Throughout the early years of the eighteenth century the pottery money box appears to have gone out of fashion, for hardly any examples from this period have survived in private or public collections in England. With the rapid expansion of the urban potteries in the late eighteenth and early nineteenth centuries, however, the money box became extremely popular once more, the potters taking a great pride in the ornament and detail applied to each individual piece. In most potteries two standards of money box were produced, the simpler being an entirely plain box, designed for sale with the remainder of the potter's everyday produce, while the more complicated varieties were made only to individual orders, in which case they usually bore some suitable inscription.

Most of the simpler money boxes followed the onion-shaped pattern of the early Surrey examples, but during the eighteenth century a number of distinct regional styles began gradually to emerge. In Surrey itself the boxes became taller, often acquiring high pedestal bases, while the original green-glazed white fabric was normally replaced by a bright red fabric covered with either an olive-green or a red-brown lead glaze. Such pieces were made by William Smith, the well-known potter of nineteenth-century Farnborough, and also by William Harris of nearby Farnham, whose grandsons continue to make them today. Throughout the midlands the early shape was continued in the various local fabrics, but in the north there was a tendency to make them rather tall in proportion to their width, as the many examples to be seen in the northern museums illustrate. In Sussex and Kent, meanwhile, money boxes in both plain red fabrics and also in red and white agate-ware fabrics tended to become rather more cylindrical in form, their sides often being constricted by a series of horizontal grooves or flanges to give a more interesting outline. Typical examples are now to be seen in the Victoria and Albert Museum (no. C 344.1919). The Brede Pottery also made them with two chambers placed one above the other to resemble a tall cottage loaf in silhouette, each chamber having its own slot to take a different coin (V and A no. C 335.1919).

On the whole the order-made pieces tend to be far more interesting than their everyday contemporaries, for not only are they made in a greater variety of shapes and styles, often enabling the potter to be identified with a fair degree of accuracy on this evidence alone, but they occasionally bear the owner's name or initials, which can be checked against such local documents as parish registers or trade directories. Frequently they are also inscribed with the date of their manufacture and the name of the locality in which their owner lived, all of which can help in tracing the former life of each individual piece. The majority of the order-made pieces were decorated with small model birds in a variety of sizes and colours, thus earning them the general title of 'hen and chickens' money boxes.

Unfortunately some of the most attractive of these boxes come from a pottery which has not yet been identified. They are beautifully made, their circular bodies being drawn up into three characteristic points by a careful folding technique, each point being tipped by a finely modelled bird, while two further birds perch on a handle of entwined strands of clay which arches over the pot to complete a particularly interesting design. One of these money boxes in the Somerset County Museum at Taunton has a pale-buff-coloured fabric covered by a light-yellow lead glaze, slight traces of red clay adhering to its base. Although they are tentatively attributed to eighteenth-century Staffordshire by some authorities, there is at present no real evidence to suggest where they were actually made.

Money boxes with a pale buff fabric and yellow glaze were

also made in the potteries of Burton-in-Lonsdale, but these are quite different in form. A fine provenanced example in the Yorkshire Museum at York (no. 76/a) has the usual onion-shaped body surmounted by a large 'hen' knob and five

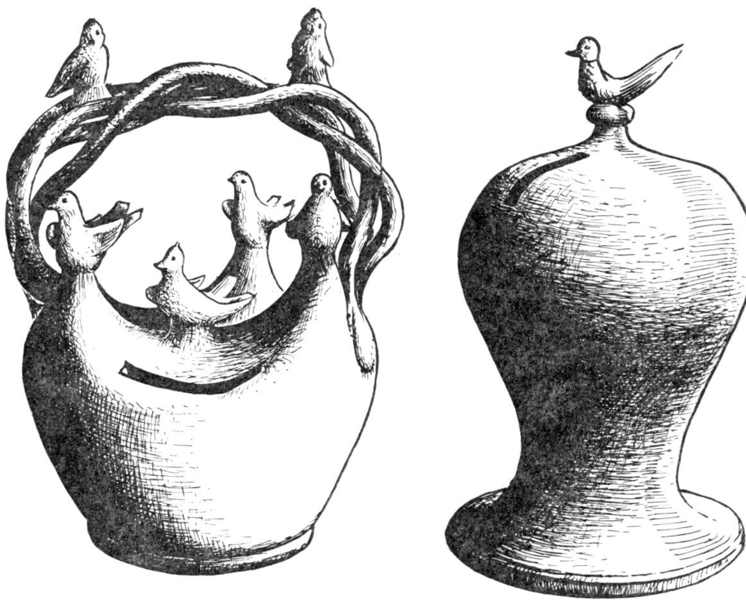

Fig 6 Money boxes from Staffordshire (?) (left) and from Leafield, Oxfordshire (right), the latter being made by George Franklin in 1905

encircling 'chickens', the birds in this case being enriched with dark-brown slip dots about their eyes, combs and wings. Two coin slots are cut through the shoulder of the pot, and beneath one of these the initials 'J.B.' are neatly pricked out in outline in the Roman lettering so characteristic of this particular potting community. According to an old label, this money box was made at Burton-in-Lonsdale in 1830, the initials presumably being those of John Bateson of the Town End Pottery, who was active here at this period.

Very similar money boxes were made at Gorsty Hill in Worcestershire, their decoration being either in black slip on a pale buff fabric or in white slip over black. They may be readily distinguished from those of Burton-in-Lonsdale, however, as their slip-trailing is far richer, and their birds are quite different in form (see page 35), with whistles concealed in their tails.

In Somerset the Donyatt potters produced a unique variety of hen and chickens box which, although retaining the usual onion-shaped body, had no terminal knob. Instead the top of the box was occupied by a large fan-tailed bird with a long neck and pointed beak. Round it, and along the edge of the bird's tail, were modelled numerous miniature chickens, each deftly pinched from a small roll of clay. One example of this type was purchased by Dr Glaisher from the descendants of a potter called Norris who made it at the Donyatt potteries in 1836; this piece is now no. 173 in the Fitzwilliam Museum's Glaisher Collection.

In most of the other English potteries rather plainer varieties of the hen and chickens money box were made, the chickens often being omitted to leave a single bird as a terminal. George Franklin made such wares at the Leafield Pottery near Burford about the turn of the century, one example of his work in the Oxford City and County Museum at Woodstock (no. 1730) having a tall onion-shaped body rising above a widely flaring foot, a single small bird perching on the thrown knob on top. At the Weatheriggs Pottery in Westmorland Mr H. Thorburn and his father also made money boxes bearing a single 'hen'. The shape of the body here was very similar to that of a stoneware bottle, having no foot, tapering sides and a domed top furnished with a knob to support the bird. Frequently the Weatheriggs money boxes are also decorated either by the addition of applied clay strips resembling narrow twigs or branches or else by dipping in either blue or green slips, so that the bird alone is left to show the true dark-red colour of the fabric itself.

In addition to these relatively small money boxes the Yorkshire potteries also made some extremely tall examples which represent some of the finest achievements of the country potter's art. Those made in the village of Burton-in-Lonsdale in north-west Yorkshire are outstanding, as the example made for 'James. Whitaker. 1938' on page 35 illustrates. The body of this box consists of a round base surmounted by a cylindrical cage and a tall conical roof from which spring eight ornamental handles to form an ornate crown terminal. Within the cage sits a perfectly modelled bird, an extremely surprising feature when it is realised that the whole body of the pot, from top to bottom, was formed on the wheel from a single lump of clay. This pot is also of particular interest, as its entire history is known. According to a family tradition, James Whitaker, master of the Kendal Bluecoat School from 1837 to 1878, ordered this money box from a Burton-in-Lonsdale potter who was visiting the Kendal Fair of 1838. The pot was delivered later and it must have proved satisfactory, for a little later an identical one was obtained from the same potter, this time bearing the inscription 'Anne. Whitaker. 1841' for James's wife. Apparently the pottery at 'Black Burton', as it was locally known, supplied quite a large area of the Lake District, for other money boxes of this type are known, bearing such inscriptions as 'T: L: Mill of Millam Cumberland 1841', 'This His a Save All 1815+', and 'Dorothy. Ann. French'.

The Hallidays of the Howcans Pottery, Halifax, also produced a number of these tall Yorkshire money boxes during the third quarter of the nineteenth century, but these were not quite up to the standard of the Burton-in-Lonsdale examples. The Yorkshire Museum Collection contains one made at Howcans in 1860 (no. 77). It is made from red and white 'snail-horn' ware clay, and consists of a low spherical base topped with a broad cylindrical body and a conical roof. The two upper sections are pierced with triangular and cross-shaped knife-cut perforations, while two borders of pinched-out red and white pigeons adorn the pot's waist and roof.

Some of the most interesting Yorkshire money boxes, however, are the miniature chests of drawers and dressers made in the Halifax region. Usually dating from the mid-nineteenth century, they are extremely well made, being built up from individual slabs of clay carefully cut to size, stuck together with slip and decorated in some detail. Perhaps the finest of these is that illustrated in Ling Roth's *Yorkshire Coiners* of 1906, figure 118. This particular example is made in agate-ware, the various slabs having been sliced off a solid block of coarsely mixed clay with a taut wire, as any attempt at rolling out would have blurred the fine markings. To shape the front of this chest of drawers the potter had made a shallow intaglio press-mould showing the edges of each drawer, the mouldings round the top and base and the pilaster sides of the framework itself. This enabled him to produce any number of well-modelled fronts with ease, saving a great deal of time and trouble. The top and sides were then added in agate ware, while the back and base were left in the plain red-firing clay. When the pot was almost dry a sharp tool was taken and the following inscription incised into the back 'LOT. SLADEN. APRIL. 27. 1846', each letter being inlaid with white clay to give a good contrast with the dark brown background. A similar inlaying technique was used to decorate the remarkable miniature dresser now housed in the Folk Museum of West Yorkshire at Shibden Hall, Halifax. This piece, mounted on four tall thrown legs and decorated with two brown pigeons along its top, was made by Elizabeth Kitson in her father's Woodman House Pottery near Elland. Across the front face, beneath the curving V-rouletted cornice, the inscription 'E K 1853 Id+Au' is inlaid in white clay, while tree and heart motifs in the same technique enrich each side panel.

At the other side of the Pennines, the Lancashire potters also made money boxes in the form of chests of drawers, but these were rather different from those of their Yorkshire contemporaries. Their fronts were press-moulded to show three large drawers and two small ones, on top of which ran a broad top rail bearing the words 'SAVINGS BANK'. The money slot, meanwhile, was situated at the top of the rear panel. Often the dark red fabric from which these pots were made was decorated with details of applied white clay. One example at

Rufford Old Hall has white knobs on the drawers and the inscription 'Jane E. Wilburn' inlaid across its back, while another in the Greg Collection at Manchester City Art Gallery (no. 1923.215) bears rows of applied white clay pellets which have been overstamped to form small seven-petalled rosettes.

Although the northern potters conformed to a fairly limited range of money-box types, those of north Devon were notable for their great variety and originality of form. The earlier boxes from this area appear to have been of the normal onion-shaped pattern, their sgraffito decoration revealing a red fabric beneath the thin coating of white slip. Typical of these is a late eighteenth-century example in the Beatson Blair Collection (no. 1947.601), at Manchester, which has leaves, flowers and birds spaced round it, with the owner's (?) initials 'G S' placed just above the coin slot. By the early nineteenth century the north Devon potters were making their money boxes as purely individual items, designing and making each one as the fancy took them. One of the most pleasing of these is now in the museum in Bideford Public Library. It is in the form of a curly-tailed dog standing on a rectangular base, the sides of which are decorated with a flower, a man with a bird, a yacht with three sailors, and the inscription 'A Trifel for John Jun 12 1821' beneath the frontal slot. Admittedly the cutting of the sgraffito could be more precise, and the dog shows little anatomical detail, but this does not matter, for such concern with minutiae would have killed the warm and human qualities in which this piece is so rich. Similar comments could be made regarding most of the north Devon money boxes, including the amusing thatched-cottage box by 'GEORGE G. FISHLEY. January 12th 1862', which forms part of the Charbonier Collection in the Exeter Museum.

Most of the so-called 'traditional English piggy banks' which are now to be had in a wide range of pastel shades, resplendent with painted daisies and pale pink bows, have a comparatively short pedigree. The first pig money boxes, to use the potter's matter-of-fact expression, appear to have originated in a number of country potteries during the last quarter of the nineteenth century. Of these two remain in production: those of the Farnham Pottery in Surrey, and those of Lake's Pottery in Truro. The Farnham examples, designed in the 1890s by

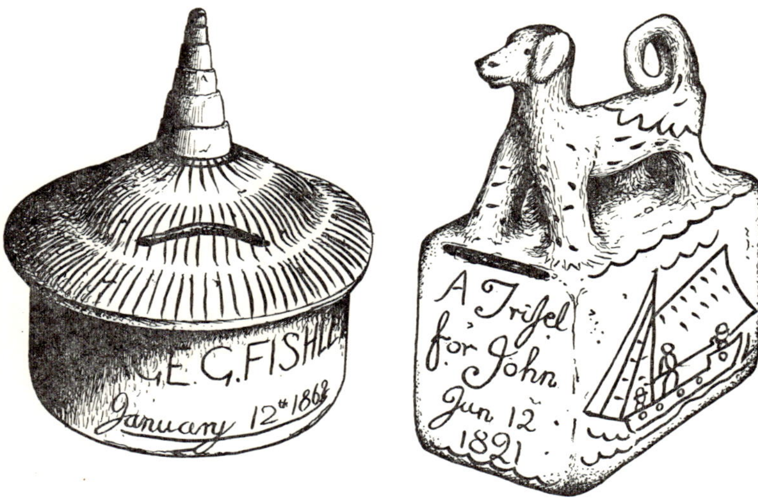


Fig 7 North Devon sgraffito money boxes by George Fishley of Fremington

William Freemantle Harris, are press-moulded from thin slabs of clay, and are usually sold in either a nut-brown or a copper-green-glazed finish. The modelling of the pig itself is extremely fine for, unlike most of today's somewhat shapeless 'piggies', it was modelled directly from an old sow, the character of which it retains beautifully. William Harris's accounts have shown that he was also a part-time farmer, owning a number of horses and spending his holidays in the hop-grounds; it is obvious that he had first-hand experience of pigs, for in no other way could he have produced such an honest yet appealing portrait, with its squatting pose and raised inquisitive snout (see page 36). Mr Lake's pigs from Truro, also designed in the 1890s, are quite different both in their design and in their method of production. Instead of being press-moulded their bodies are skilfully thrown on the wheel, the eyes, front trotters and so on all being modelled on by hand later. The form of the thrown section is admirably devised to fit the pig's contours, and such small details as the knife-curl of the underlip or the twisting of the ears show that sensitive blend of good craftsmanship with knowledgeable design so typical of the English earthenware money box.

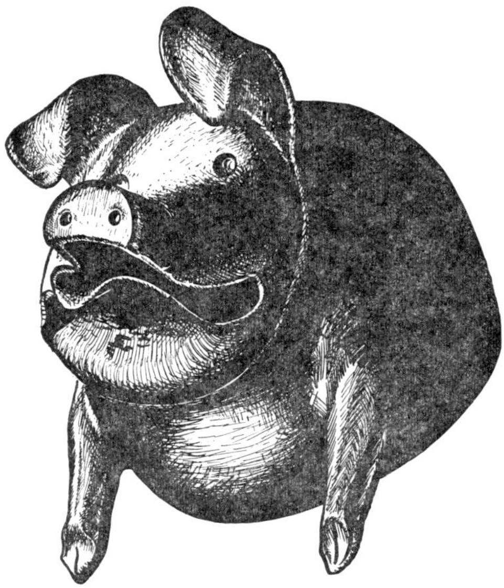

Fig 8 A Truro pig money box of the 1890s

*Notes for this chapter are on page 178*

## *Chapter Four*

# *Harvest Wares*

The provision of suitable liquid refreshment at harvest time has always been a matter of considerable importance to the English countryman, understandably so when it is remembered that he had to spend long hours swinging a scythe, sickle or fagging hook in the fields during the full heat of summer. Although cider, water or, later, cold tea could be used to quench his thirst, the normal harvest drink was beer, its quality and strength depending on the farmer who brewed it. Usually quite weak new beer was supplied, one which could be drunk in great quantities without having much effect on the senses. As a Sussex labourer told the Rector of Harting in the late nineteenth century, it was such that he 'never knew a man drunk in the harvest field in my life. Could drink six quarts; and believe that a man might [drink] two gallons in a day.'[1] In some areas a stronger brew was obtainable, as indicated by the comment of a Shropshire man: 'They'n got some 'o the best owd beer at Goff o' Wes'ley as ever I tasted ... they wun al'ays noted for good aroost-drink.'[2] Whatever the nature of the drink, a vessel had to be devised to ensure its safe transport into the fields. In some areas small coopered barrels or black leather flasks were used for this purpose, but in most parts of the country the ceramic harvest jug, flask or costrel predominated. Many of these pots epitomised the concept of good design flowing from functional necessity alone, the bold spherical forms, simple decoration and strong applied details of the Sussex and Dorset wares illustrating this particularly well. Other harvest wares provided the country potters with a unique opportunity to develop their traditional techniques of decoration.

Of the plainer harvest wares the most common are undoubtedly the buff-bodied and yellow-glazed jugs and costrels made at Verwood in eastern Dorset (see page 71). Variously known as either Dorset pills, from their rotund bodies, or 'owls' from the eye-like appearance of their lugs, the costrels were used by the agricultural labourers of Dorset, Hampshire and Wiltshire from the early nineteenth century at least. Examples are still to be found in these counties, some, like those from Selborne (now in the Hampshire County Museum Collection), coming to light in the fields, where they were apparently forgotten many years ago. In form, all the Verwood costrels are alike, having an almost spherical body rising from a plain convex base-mould to a narrow, slightly flaring neck into which a cork might be driven. Just below the neck two small semi-circular lugs are applied, their upper edges being pinched to a scalloped outline and their centres pierced with either one or two holes to take the cord for suspension. Often the costrels are finished in this state, but occasionally a number of encircling grooves are incised round their shoulders as a simple form of decoration, while inscriptions such as 'Lion Brewery, Salisbury' are very rarely added in a free copperplate hand.[3] The Verwood jugs, meanwhile, are extremely plain, well-proportioned vessels, having a smooth S-shaped profile as their bulbous bodies rise from a simple rounded base-moulding to a widely flaring mouth. The coarse fabrics, crude lead glazes and strong forms of these wares led many people to believe that they are medieval, but, rather surprisingly, they were still being made in the traditional manner from foot-trodden clay on hand-turned wheels by Mesech Sims of Verwood up to the early 1950s.

Further along the south coast, in Sussex, harvest wares with similar strong shapes were made in the rich dark red iron-flecked fabric of that county. Some of the most attractive of these are also the most simple, the colour and texture of their materials alone being sufficient to give them great beauty.

Notable among these wares is a group of bottles made during the opening years of the nineteenth century. These pots have spherical bodies, which usually show a slight flattening across their tops before they arise to their almost cylindrical necks and small looped strap handles. Even though most bottles of this type are completely plain, a number of them do bear minimal strips of decoration round their shoulders. One bottle in the Worthing Museum, for example, has two narrow bands of inlaid white clay in this position, between which runs the inscription: 'X R YOUNG X SHEFFEL X ARMS X 14 X', while a further example is known to have been made for the marriage of 'CHARLES AND HARRIOT MOREN WARDHURST SUSSEX JUNE 3 1819'.

Unlike those made in other parts of the country, the majority of the harvest wares made in Sussex were neither jugs nor bottles, but instead took the form of smaller kegs or flasks. The most usual ones to have survived are the kegs which closely copied the shape and proportions of the rather elongated cane-bound casks of oak, which had been made by the coopers of the southern counties from the mid-eighteenth century. Round each end of these kegs an appropriate number of raised bands was thrown to represent the cane bindings, a coating of white slip giving them a more realistic appearance. Their necks, meanwhile, were knife cut from rectangular blocks of clay in imitation of their wooden prototypes, rather than following the normal circular designs of thrown pottery. The probable reasons for their relatively high rate of survival are twofold: firstly, their small size and strong serviceable shapes made accidental breakages rare; secondly, their high quality and the practice of inscribing them with their owner's names has ensured their preservation throughout the succeeding generations. Many of these wares appear to have been made from the late eighteenth century at the Brede Pottery, for one in the Glaisher Collection (no. 338) is inscribed 'THOMAS MUNN BENENDEN KENT. AUGUST 27.1800', Benenden being ten miles north of Brede. Another at the Hastings Museum bears the initials 'W.A. 1821' for William Apps, who died at Brede in 1867 at the age of eighty-two, while a further example in the British Museum (no. Q6) states that it was made for 'MRS CASSAM. A PRESENT FROM HER NIECE SARAH FRANCES YOUNG, BREDE, SUSSEX, 1829'. It is likely that these kegs were made in other local potteries, too, for one in the City of Stoke-on-Trent's Museum at Hanley marked: 'D + M 1843', 'Here's to thee my honest Frend Wishing these hard times to mend', is attributed to Rye, although on what grounds is not certain.

The other variety of vessel to be produced in Sussex was the spirit flask. This was rather like a large pocket-watch in form, with slightly convex circular sides and a small projecting mouthpiece on one edge. This shape left the potter with two ideal surfaces on which to inlay his decoration, an opportunity he did not intend to miss. Even on some of the earliest flasks, such as the one in the museum at Stoke-on-Trent which was made for 'WILLIAM VIDEAN/BOUGHTON/JULY 27th/ 1796' were lines such as these:

AN EPITATH
SHALL WE ALL DIE
WE SHALL DIE ALL
ALL DIE SHALL WE
DIE ALL WE SHALL

The Siggery family were among the first to make these wares, probably their earliest surviving flask being one made at the Boship Pottery, Lower Dicker, by John Siggery in 1794 (Victoria and Albert Museum, no. C349–1919). It is inscribed 'Otions of Brandy And Rivers of Wine Plantecion of Tea & a Garle To my mind'. Another of his flasks, this time in the Glaisher Collection (no. 357), informs us that it was 'MADE BY JOHN SIGGERY POTTER WISTOW SUSSEX' 'FOR WILLIAM TERRY APSLEE THAKEHAM SUSSEX OCTR 7 1812', 'COME JOVAL FELLOWS DRINK ABOUT WE, I HAVE MORE WHEN THIS IS OUT'. A further John Siggery, probably the son of the above, made very similar pieces at Hurstmonceux in the 1830s, but his spelling was slightly improved, as is seen on a flask (Glaisher Collection, no. 358) 'GIVEN TO EMMA GOLDSMITH [his future wife] BATTLE SUSSEX 1835'. On one side this flask reads:

ORCANS
OF BRANDY
RIVERS OF WINE
FOUNTAINS OF
TEA & A GIRL
TO MY MIND

and along the edge 'MADE BY JOHN SIGGERY HERSTMON$^{x}$ SUSSEX'. At Chailey, the potters tended to extol the virtues of their flasks' contents in beautifully inlaid and ornamented panels of rhyme. One made for 'SAM$^{1}$. WATERS. CRANBROOK. 1800' at 'SOUTH CHAILEY POTTERY' boasts that;

Wine cheers the heart,
and warms the blood
and at this season's migh
ty good

(Glaisher Collection no. 356), while another (British Museum no. Q8), made here by 'RICHARD NORMAN', invites 'OF LIQUOR GOOD FRIEND TAKE YOUR SHARE, AND DRINK SUCCESS TO NORMAN'S WARE, MAY 3, 1842', one side being decorated with a clock-like face bearing the inscription:

This little bottle holds a drop,
That will your drooping spirits prop,
It is strong liquor choice and good,
'Twill cheer the heart and warm the blood.

The attractive quality of these flasks has caused them to be extensively copied, and the inlaid dates are not always to be trusted. Pieces dated to the late eighteenth century and marked either 'Old Sussex Ware' or 'DICKER POTTERY', for

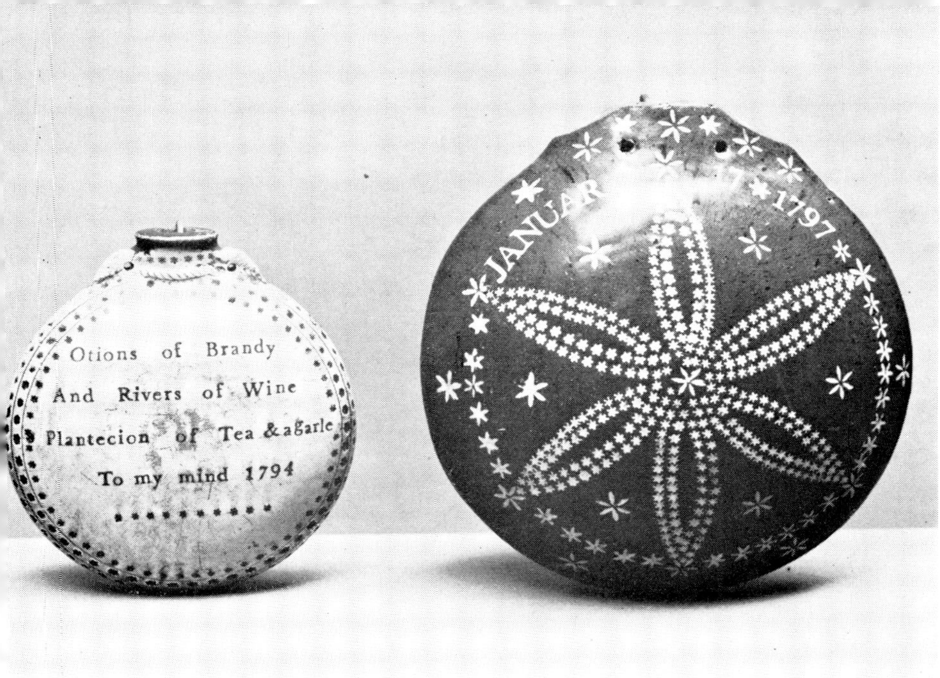


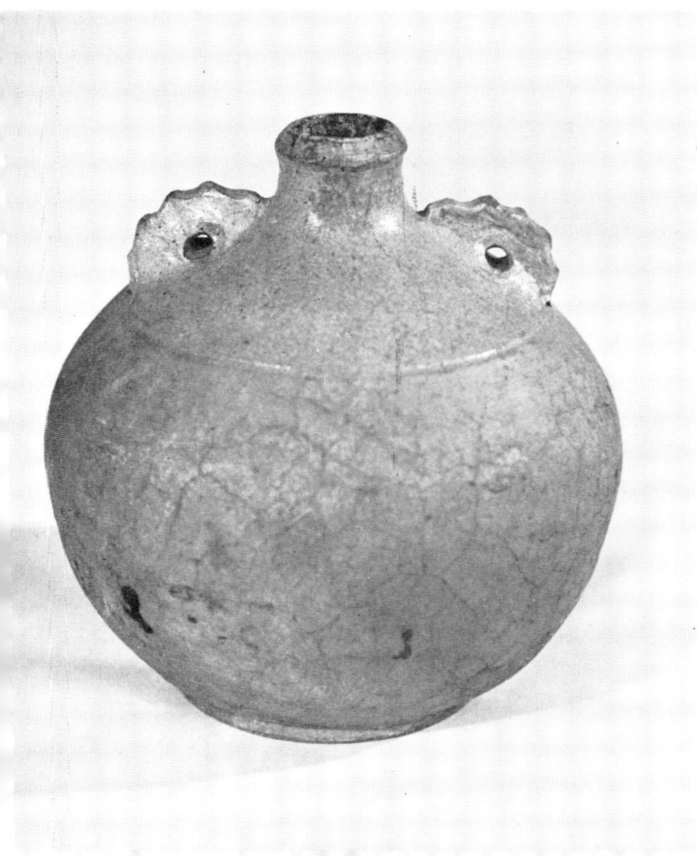

*Page 71* Harvest wares, the Sussex flasks (*above*) having fine inlaid decoration of an extremely high standard, in contrast to the severely utilitarian pills or owls of nineteenth-century Verwood in the New Forest (*left*) (see notes on pages 182–3)

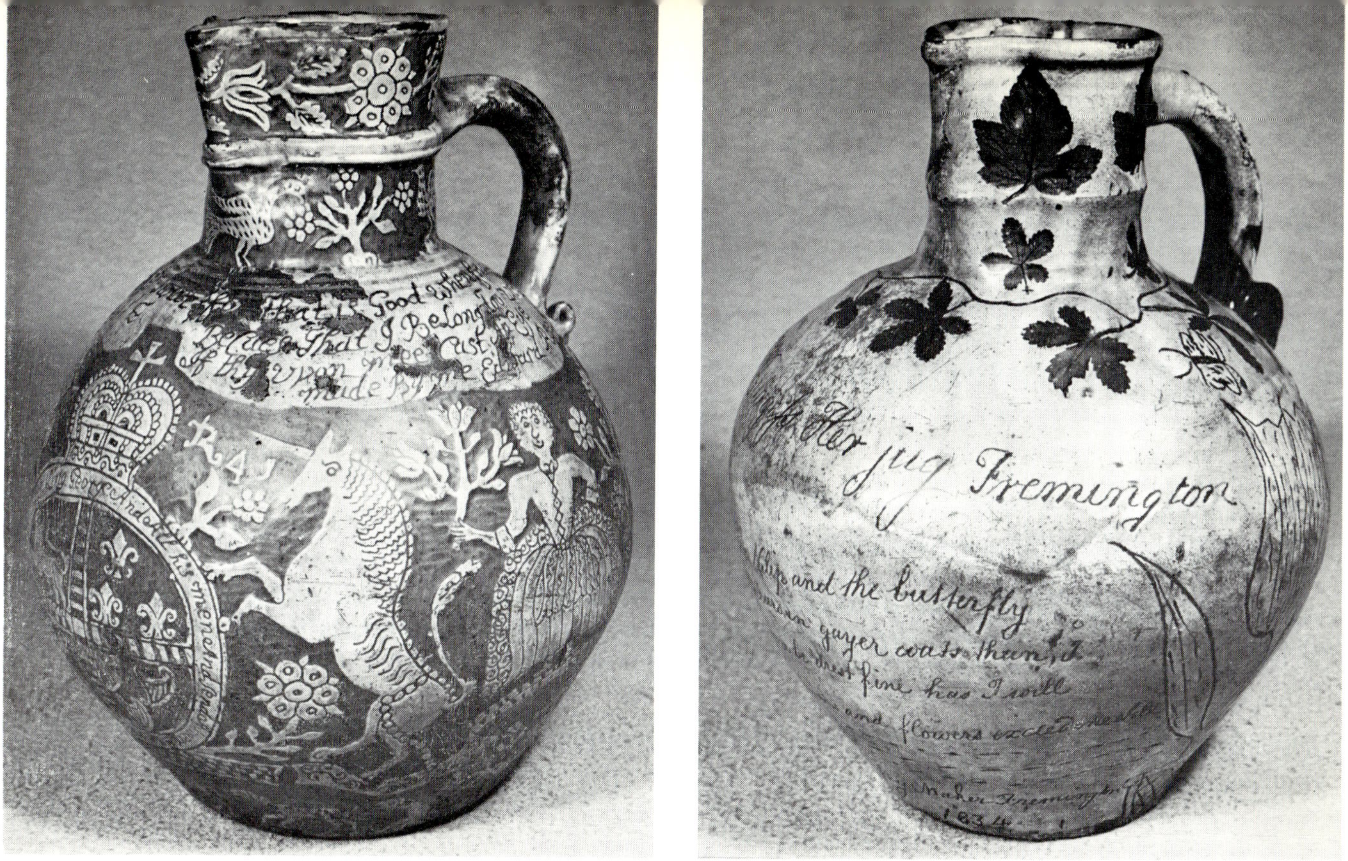


*Page 72* North Devon harvest jugs, one being made by Edward Reed and decorated by Thomas Stonman on 27 June 1741 (*left*), while the other was produced by Robert Fishley of Fremington in 1834 (*right*) (see notes on page 183)

example, are almost certainly of early twentieth-century date, being made as reproductions for the unscrupulous dealer and the unwary collector.

The most magnificent English harvest wares were undoubtedly those made in the potteries of the north Devon coast from the mid-seventeenth century. Unlike the majority of their contemporaries these jugs were decorated in a most elaborate manner in the sgraffito technique with a red fabric and creamy-white slip, their surfaces being covered in plant, animal or figure designs accompanied by numerous inscriptions and rhymes. Besides being used to carry ale, cider or water these jugs appear to have been used in an almost ceremonial manner for 'crying the neck', a custom observed in many parts of the west country when the final sheaf, or neck, was cut from the harvest field when:

> The reaper, with his reaping hook (it was thought a shame to cut wheat with any other tool) having cut a last handful of wheat, held and waved it high over his head, as with a loud and joyful voice he cried 'I have et, I have et, I have et', on which the other harvesters standing around shouted 'What have 'e?, What have 'e?, What have 'e?', and then arose the triumphant cry 'A NEK, A NEK, A NEK HOORAA'.[4]

Hone, in his *Everyday Book* of 1826 (p 155), also gives a description of this custom in Devonshire, where: 'Our people were harvesting, I heard six or seven "necks" cried in one night, although I know that some of them were four miles off. They are heard at great distances sometimes.' Following the crying of the neck the harvesters returned to celebrate the end of harvest in a rather pleasant manner with the maximum consumption of ale and cider, at which the jugs undoubtedly played an important part. This is amply shown by the inscription on a north Devon jug now in the City Museum, Plymouth, which states that:

> The Potter fashioned me complete,
> as plainly doth appear
> for to supply the harvest men with
> good strong English beer

Drink round my jolly reapers and
When the corn is cut we'll have
the other jug boys and cry
A Neck A Neck.

Able Symons 1813.

Some of the jugs were also made as presents, or perhaps even as love tokens, their inscriptions recording that they were made for someone to present to a member of the opposite sex, as will be seen on a number of the jugs described below.

The production of the large harvest jugs appears to have begun in the second half of the seventeenth century, the earliest recognisable group having bold outline designs cut into the red fabrics through overall coatings of white slip.[5] Probably the earliest example of this type is a jug dated 1698 and mentioned in E. A. Barber's *Lead Glazed Pottery* of 1908 (p 12) as being in an American collection. This fine piece, formerly used in Sussex County, Delaware, bears a female bust above an oval cartouche, supported by unicorns and a swan, the former motif being the chief characteristic of the whole group. The upper portion of this jug is inscribed:

Kind Sr: i com to Gratifiey youre Kindness Love and
and Courtisy and Sarve youre table with Strong beare
  for thes
intent i was sent heare; or if you pleas i will supply
  your workmen when in
harvist dry when they doe labour hard and sweate
  good drink is better far then Meat.

Further examples dating from the opening decades of the eighteenth century are to be seen in the Glaisher Collection, in the Fitzwilliam Museum, Cambridge. They too have the female bust motif, but they also depict thistles, unicorns, birds, tulips and hearts in outline round their bodies. Typical examples include nos. 58, 59 and 61 in this collection, the former being dated 1700 within a cartouche and inscribed round the upper section of the body:

> now i am com for to supply your workmen when in
> haruist dry when thy doe labour harde and sweat
> good drink
> is better far than meate: in winter time when it is
> coold i likewise
> then good drinke can hould: booth seasons doe the
> same require and most
> men doe good drinke desire.

No. 59 bears a very similar rhyme and is dated 'WH 1724'. while no. 60, resplendent with a heart and crossed arrows, reads;

> I S cupids Dart wounded my hart 1728
> When you your frinds you do invite there hearts and
> for to chear
> O then i pray make use of me and fill me with strong
> beer
> And when that you together sit your selves for to divert
> Then fill your cup and drink about a health with all
> your heart.

From at least the opening of the eighteenth century a number of north Devon potters began to decorate their large harvest jugs by scratching away the areas of slip between each individual decorative feature to leave their white slip designs standing slightly proud of the red background, this being a considerable improvement on the earlier outline work. A fairly early example of this is to be seen in the Willet Collection in the British Museum, where a jug (no. D115) decorated with large figures and flowers is dated 1708. In addition, a number of potters developed individual styles of decoration by which their wares may be readily distinguished from those of other potters, such details as the choice of rhyme or subject or the techniques of representation providing much useful material on which to base attributions. In some of these wares, however, care has to be taken in deciding who carried out the decoration, for it was not always executed by the person who made the pot itself. Evidence for this is given on an extremely fine jug in the City Museum, Stoke-on-Trent (no. 304 P40). On this example the motifs include the royal arms, a lady and gentlemen in eighteenth-century dress, a deer hunt with deer, hounds and huntsmen, and a number of bird and flower borders. The inscription reads;

> G. R. 1741
> God Bles King George And All his men
> And send Admerell Vernon home A Gain
> Come fill mee full with Licker sweet for that is good when frends doo meet
> make noo Delay but fill mee quick Be Caus That I Belong Too Week
> And I will treat my frends As thy pas By If thy upon mee Cast An Eye
> Drane by me Thomas Stonman June 27
> Made by me Edward Reed.

The majority of the nineteenth-century potters appear to have both made and decorated their wares in person as a matter of pride, although craftsmen specialising as decorators were occasionally employed during the latter half of the century, when art wares were being made in large quantities. The following are probably the most important of the north Devon sgraffito ware jug makers to work during this period.

*John Bird*

This potter, listed in Pigot's 1830 *Directory* as being of Potter's Lane, Bideford, is particularly characterised by his use of large crudely cut lions on his decorative wares. These may be recognised quite easily by such details as the lion's crown, which is composed of two intersecting semi-circles with scalloped internal border (see page 108), its mouth, in the form of an elongated ellipse regularly divided into small rectangular teeth, and its tail, which expands to an almost balloon-like terminal. Examples of his work are now to be seen in the Royal Albert Memorial Museum, Exeter, where a harvest jug (no. 74/1931/2) bears one of his typical lions between floral designs and the rhyme:

> Drink round my Jovial
> fellows and when that
> this is done well have
> the other jug my Boys
> and sing a Mery song
> August 25 1818 Wm Ough Quathiock.

*C. H. Brannam*

C. H. Brannam of the North Walk and Litchdon Street potteries in Barnstaple was apparently a maker of first-class north Devon sgraffito jugs, for in 1851 he received a bronze medal and also the compliments of Prince Albert when he exhibited six of his productions at the Crystal Palace exhibition. The North Devon Athenaeum in Barnstaple possesses a signed example in red-line sgraffito ware. Round the upper half of the body are arranged groups of flowers and grass, while the area below shows a number of fish swimming in the sea.

*Philip Burch*

In the Glaisher Collection (no. 71) is a Barnstaple jug decorated across the front with a large sun face between bushes of roses and tulips, while at the rear are two medallion faces, and two peacocks with a small bird in a rectangular panel in which is inscribed:

> Humphrey Whitefield 1788 Philip Burch Maker 1788
> Now I'm come for to supply
> Good Harvestmen when they are Dry
> BARUM 1788.

*George Fishley (1771–1865)*

Although George Fishley of Fremington Pottery was one of the most prolific and interesting potters of the nineteenth century, very few of his harvest jugs appear to have survived in public collections. Those which have survived show a wealth of decorative detail in sgraffito and applied motifs. Typical of these is a signed jug now in the Bideford Library Museum, which fully demonstrates his patriotic sentiments. Round the body a white ensign is seen to fly above the French tricolour, while the stamp showing Napoleon, usually associated with his ornamental watch-pockets, is firmly placed beneath the lip of the spout. Further decorative features cut in outline through a coating of white slip include tulips and birds in foliage, while round the neck extends a border of small palmate leaves in resist. Care has to be taken in attributing unsigned pieces of stamped sgraffito ware to George Fishley, for the use of his moulds and stamps is no guarantee of his workmanship. Succeeding members of his family often used his old tools to decorate their products, as is seen below.

*Edmund Fishley (d. 1861)*

Edmund Fishley, George's son, made a number of harvest jugs from the 1820s onwards, most of their designs being executed in red sgraffito linework. A typical feature of his wares is the use of a heart-shaped cartouche to contain an inscription, these usually being placed beneath the lower joint of the handle, although they occasionally occur across the front of the pot, just above its widest point. He apparently restricted himself to the use of four rhymes on his wares, three of these being used on a signed presentation jug in the Royal Albert Memorial Museum, Exeter (no. 7/1927.4). This reads:

1. Edmund Fishley Maker Fremington June 6 1839
   Wm. Mildon, Halswell, Chittlehampton, 1839
   The tulip and the butterfly
   Appear in gayer coats than I
   Let me be dress'd fine as I will
   Flies, worms, and flowers exceed me still.

2. This little Jug
in Friedship take
And keep it for
the givers sake
Rebecca Searle
June 6 1839.

3. Long may you live
Happy may you be
Bless with content
And from misfortunes
Free.

To take up the theme of the first rhyme this jug bears suitable illustrations of tulips and butterflies round its sides. The fourth rhyme occurs on a jug in the Glaisher Collection (no. 81), where a man smoking a pipe is accompanied by the inscription:

4. Despise me not
Be Cause Im smol
Fel me often hil
Ples you
All
Edmund Fishley Maker 1824

*Robert Fishley*

Robert Fishley produced very similar wares to those of his brother Edmund, their rhymes, decorations and dates being almost identical. Robert often tended to have rather weaker spelling than his brother, as is shown by the following rhyme from a signed example in the Glaisher Collection (no. 82);

Richd & Mary Dinnis Monkleigh May 12 1836
The tulip and the butter Fly
Appears in gayer tints Than I
let me be drest Fine as [I will]
Flise worms and Flours exceed me still.

In addition, his red sgraffito linework tends to be cruder and more varied in its subjects. One of his early signed jugs in the City Museum, Stoke-on-Trent (no. 242 P40) illustrates a bird, a fish, some flowers, the Duke of Wellington, an olive branch and a number of Union Jacks, together with the rhyme 'Long life and/Success to the/Farmer/1819' in a heart-shaped cartouche beneath the handle. A further jug in the Royal Albert Memorial Museum, Exeter (no. 100/1930) shows a man ploughing, a head within a palm wreath, a group of trees, a view of a cottage complete with two men and a cow and the inscription:

> He that by the Plough would thrive
> Himself must either hold or drive.
>
> March 3rd R. FISHLEY, Jug.

Sometimes Robert used his father's stamps and moulds to decorate his own wares, this being illustrated by a fine jug in the Burton Art Gallery, Bideford (no. 272). In addition to versions of the second, third and fourth rhymes used by Edmund and the owner's name ('Tristram Gint/Torrington/December 6th 1846'), it bears a group of three circular stamped rosettes and two acorns pressed from George Fishley's moulds to provide an elaborate and unique terminal to the lower handle joint. A similar use of George's moulds is to be seen in the Glaisher Collection (no. 83), where a small jug made by Robert as a present for John Murch to give to Sarah Gregory bears the typical face mask so often seen on his father's watch-pockets. Robert also adopted his father's technique of using small palmate leaves to form resist patterns in the white slip round the necks of his jugs, this being found on an example in the City Museum, Stoke-on-Trent (no. 322 P50) made by him for Susan Burgess of Fremington on 25 April 1834.

*Edwin Beer Fishley (d. 1911)*

Following in the family tradition, Edwin Beer Fishley took over the ownership of the Fremington Pottery on the death of his grandfather in 1865. During the next forty-six years he proceeded to make the widest possible range of wares, constantly adopting new styles, materials and techniques to enable the pottery to survive the rapidly changing economic and aesthetic climate of the nineteenth century. Despite the necessity to bring his wares up to date, he continued to produce a number of harvest jugs in the typical Fremington red-line sgraffito. Unlike his father and uncle, Edwin Fishley did not adopt many of George Fishley's stylistic features, though he frequently made use of old Fremington rhymes. Most of his harvest jugs bear the pronounced motif of a large circular cartouche of laurel leaf scratched through the slip beneath the spout, this being used to enclose the name of his patron and the date.

A typical specimen of this type is now in the Royal Albert Memorial Museum at Exeter (no. 89/1928.8). Inside its laurel-wreath cartouche is the inscription 'James Harris/Slade Farm /August 5th 1868', with 'E. B. Fishley, Fremington, N. Devon' beneath. To the left it reads:

> Success to the farmer,
> The plough and the flail,
> May the landlord ever flourish,
> And the tenant never fail.

To the right is the customary:

> Long may you live
> Happy may you be
> Blest with content
> and from missfortunes free

while under the handle appears:

> Despise me not because I'm small
> Fill me often I'll please you all.

The Burton Art Gallery at Bideford possesses a very similar piece (no. 227), while a further example in Barnstaple's North

Devon Athenaeum has '1881/John M. Miller/Raleigh House /Filton/Barnstaple' within its round cartouche of four encircling zig-zag lines. Besides the 'Success to the farmer' rhyme, this also wishes:

Good luck to the hoof and the horn
Good luck to the flock and the fleece
Good luck to the growers of corn
May we always have plenty and PEACE.

A number of Edwin Fishley's jugs were either decorated in person by those who ordered them or else executed to their designs. A jug in the Glaisher Collection at the Fitzwilliam Museum, Cambridge (no. 84) is of the former variety, bearing sgraffito convolvulus, foliage and butterfly motifs. Beneath its base are the signatures of E. B. Fishley and H. Potter, the latter presumably being the clergyman who, according to the vendor, originally executed the decoration in about 1880. Unfortunately no wares executed by Edwin Fishley to his patron's designs have survived in public collections, but the descriptions of them in contemporary publications suggests that they were remarkable, to say the least. Following the successful showing of his wares at the Plymouth Art and Industrial Exhibition of 1881, where he won a bronze medal, and the Newton Abbot Art Exhibition of 1882, where he was awarded the Silver Trophy, he attracted the attention of a number of wealthy patrons. One of the most important of these was Sir John Waldrond, for whom he made vessels depicting such events as 'the wedding of Bellerophon to the daughter of the Lysean monarch' and 'Bellerophon destroying the monster called the Chimaera, the glorious god being mounted on the winged horse, Pegasus, received from Minerva'. But these were a far cry from the established north Devon sgraffito harvest wares he was still making to within a week of his death in the autumn of 1911.

### *W. Fishley Holland (1889–1970)*

Fishley Holland joined the Fremington Pottery in 1902, and

became its manager following the death of his grandfather, Edwin Beer Fishley. When the pottery was sold to a Staffordshire firm in 1912 he moved to Braunton, establishing the Braunton Pottery there before moving on to Clevedon in Somerset in 1921. Compared to the earlier wares made by his family, Fishley Holland's sgraffito harvest jugs are rather soft in outline, neat in finish and glossy in glaze. Their handles, always beautifully 'pulled', have a single scroll at their base, and are topped with an applied pad or 'thumb-bit' of clay which makes them more comfortable to grip. A good example of his work made at the Clevedon Pottery in about 1930 has a broad band of white slip passing completely around it just beneath the neck. On this is inscribed the rhyme:

> Fill me full of Liquor sweet for that is good when
> friends do meet.
> When friends do meet and liquor plenty. Fill me again
> when I.B.M.T.

*Samuel Hollamore*

A jug inscribed 'Made at Samuel Hollamore's Barnstaple 1764' was sold at Sotheby's on 6 July 1933, this being the only example of his ware recorded to date.

*John Philips Hoyle*

One of the better-known north Devon potters, John Philips Hoyle worked at Crocker's Pottery, Bideford, throughout the 1850s and 1860s. Most of his wares have the neck decorated with an encircling pattern of leaves attached in pairs to a horizontal stalk, below which is a broad zig-zag design enriched with a number of vertical strokes (see page 89). Between this and the bottom handle joint there extends a panel of cross-hatching, while the base of the handle joint itself is usually decorated with a half-rose pattern. The bodies of the jugs most frequently bear such nautical motifs as ships in full sail, Union Jacks, anchors, mariner's compasses or the sun and moon, although large plant pots and birds in flowering trees are also represented on a few of his pieces. Two of his jugs showing ships in full sail are now in the Glaisher Collection (nos. 74 and 75) (see page 89), while a third is in the Bideford Library Museum. Their respective inscriptions read:

> Bucton Castle crossing the Line
> From Rocks & Sands & Every Ill may God Protect
> the Sailor Still
> John Phillips Hoyle 1857 Bideford.
>
> Sarah Newman 1860 John Hoyle Bideford 1860.
>
> Elizabeth Coop/Ocean Queen/1862.

His other designs, bearing large flower pots on their fronts, may be seen in the Royal Albert Memorial Museum, Exeter (no. 74/1931.1) and at the Weston Park Museum, Sheffield (no. k99.45), the former being inscribed:

> Miss Ann Williams
> 1866
> Paul may Plant
> and Appolos water
> But God gives
> me increase
> Bideford
> 1866

while the latter states plainly 'John Phillips Hoyle, Bideford'.

*John Phillips*

For some time a group of late eighteenth-century north Devon jugs bearing stylistically similar decorations have been recognisable to collectors, but only recently has it been possible to connect them positively and to offer any suggestion as to their maker. This development has been due to the discovery of a jug in the North Devon Athenaeum at Barnstaple. This magnificent vessel, some 15in high, is decorated with the complete range of the potter's motifs, which include the royal coat of arms with supporters and motto; a mariner's compass supported by mermaids and sea-cows; the sun in splendour; a three-masted ship; and fishes (see page 89). In addition, this Bideford potter's jugs may also be recognised by the omission of the vertical strokes in the upper triangles of the neck borders, in the dotted cross-hatching extending between the neck and the lower handle joint, or the placing of the rhyme in a heart-shaped cartouche beneath the handle. The Barnstaple Athenaeum jug also bears the following inscription:

When was in my native place
I was a Lumpe of Clay
And Digged up out of the Earth
And brought from thens a way
But now a jug I am become
By Potters Art and Skill
And I your servant am became
And Carie Ale I will
John Phillips
1760.

On the handle is the additional name 'Thomas Fields'. Three more examples of his work are in the Royal Albert Memorial Museum, Exeter. No. 38/1950 bears the royal coat of arms with supporters, motto and garter, with the rhyme:

Harvest is com all Bissey
Now in Mackin of your
Barley Mow when men do
Laber hard and swet good
Ale is bether far than meet
Bideford April 28th
1775 M & W.

No. 64/1928 bears a compass, mermaids and sea cows with:

Come fill me
full and Drinke
a bout and Never
Leave till all is out
and if that will not
make you merry
fill me again
and sing Down
Derry 1766

while no. 83/1928 bears similar motifs in addition to a two-masted ship and:

Work on Brave
Boys and never fear
You shall have ale,
Cyder and Beer, Beef
pork and pudding as I
thinke is Rear good
Eating with Strong
Drinke
1771.

In the other western counties the harvest wares tended to be much plainer in character, those of Cornwall being simple single-handled pitchers of up to 2gal capacity, each having a tall swelling body tapering swiftly above its shoulder to a deep, almost rectangular moulding about its mouth. Decoration here is often confined to a single incised line which runs round the unglazed exterior of the pot just on the shoulder-line, although the glazed rim may occasionally be given a dipped coating of contrasting white slip. The majority of the jugs from Somerset were also rather plain in comparison to those of north Devon, but a comparatively small group of competently designed pieces were made at Donyatt in the early nineteenth century. Decorated in red sgraffito line-work cut through an overall coating of white slip, they have four or five spiral scroll motifs regularly spaced round their cylindrical necks, and a running scroll border across their shoulders. Below, inscribed in a continuous spiral band which slowly descends their almost spherical bodies, are long inscriptions, such as this one, copied from a jug in the Somerset County Museum:

> In harvest time when work is hard
> Into the field I must be Carr: d
> Full of Good Cyder or Strong Beer
> your thirsty work folks for to cheer
> but If you Do Leave me at home
> but Little work There will be done
> for work is hard and Days are Long
> I hope your Liqure will be strong.

In the north and midlands the large harvest jug so common in the southern counties becomes quite rare, its place being taken by the smaller 'forenoon drinking bottle' with its 2pt or 3pt capacity. Many of these bottles follow a common pattern with rounded bodies, small necks, single handles and coarse red fabrics glazed half-way down with black iron-stained glazes. It is virtually impossible to attribute such wares to any particular pottery without some form of internal provenance (such as an old label or reliable information from the vendor), for they were made in extremely large quantities in almost every pottery from the midlands northwards. In some areas different types of slip decoration were used, however, and thus it is occasionally possible to attribute a piece to its place of manufacture by comparing it with documented specimens.

A particularly characteristic group of drinking bottles collected from the immediate locality of the Midhope Pottery during the opening years of the twentieth century now forms the Kenworthy Collection in the Sheffield City Museum. One of the most interesting ranges of coarse pottery to have survived in the north, it contains a number of the simple bottles described above, their bases here being left with the scars showing where they were sliced from the wheel with a taut wire. Instead of being left plain these 10in-high bottles are individually decorated with the initials of their owners, the copper-plate style capitals being trailed within a border of white slip. Typical inscriptions are 'M: : H 1780' (no. K1921–48), 'G.J.G.' (no. 1921–52), this being made for J. Gill of Gill Royd, Midhope, and 'W.G.' (no. 1921–50), made for Mr W. Grayson. In addition, the Midhope Pottery made forenoon drinking bottles which closely followed the shape of early eighteenth-century glass examples with short slightly tapering bodies which contract rapidly from their shoulders to join tall, almost cylindrical necks. Most of this type (such as no. K 1921–49 and two others in Wakefield City Museum) are made from a light buff-firing fabric and have been dipped neck down into a tub of iron-rich purple-brown slip to within ½in of their bases, before being covered in an overall coating of a pale-yellow lead glaze. These too are decorated with their owner's initials, here contained within a triangular border of zig-zagging lines of white slip.

At Silkstone, 5 miles north-east of Midhope, the potters made large spherical bottles with narrow necks reminiscent of those from Sussex, but lacking their fine colour and glaze. The Silkstone bottles have a dark-red fabric covered to within a few inches of the base with a near-black glaze, and bear inscriptions such as dates and initials trailed inside single rings of white slip. A provenanced example in the Cawthorne Village Museum near Barnsley bears 'P: E 1777'.

The only other identifiable harvest wares to be made in the north were the flasks produced during the late eighteenth century in the Halifax area, these wares usually having a brick-red fabric which shows as a rich red-amber beneath a warm yellow lead glaze. The flasks were first thrown to a tall ovoid silhouette, with narrow convex mouldings round their bases and short, slightly flaring mouths. While they were still plastic, two pierced lugs were added above the shoulder, and

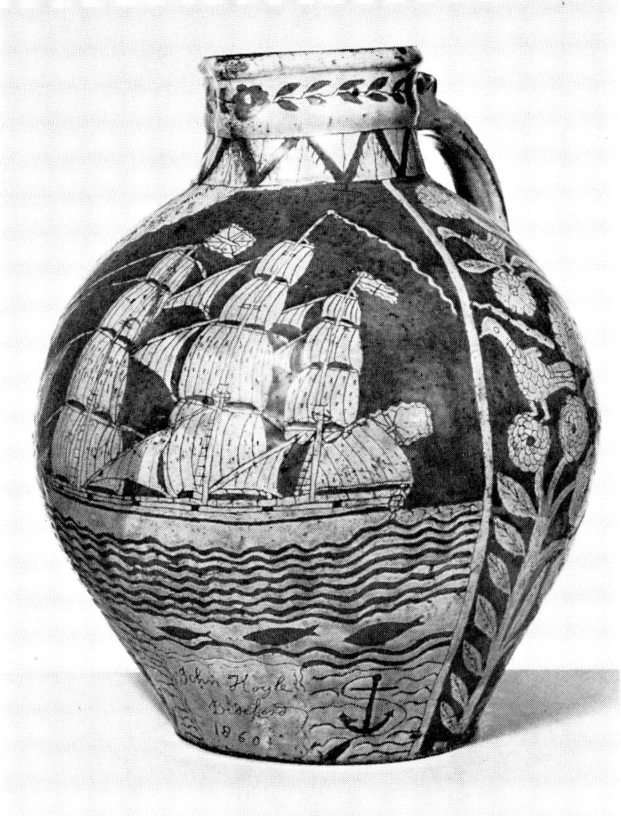


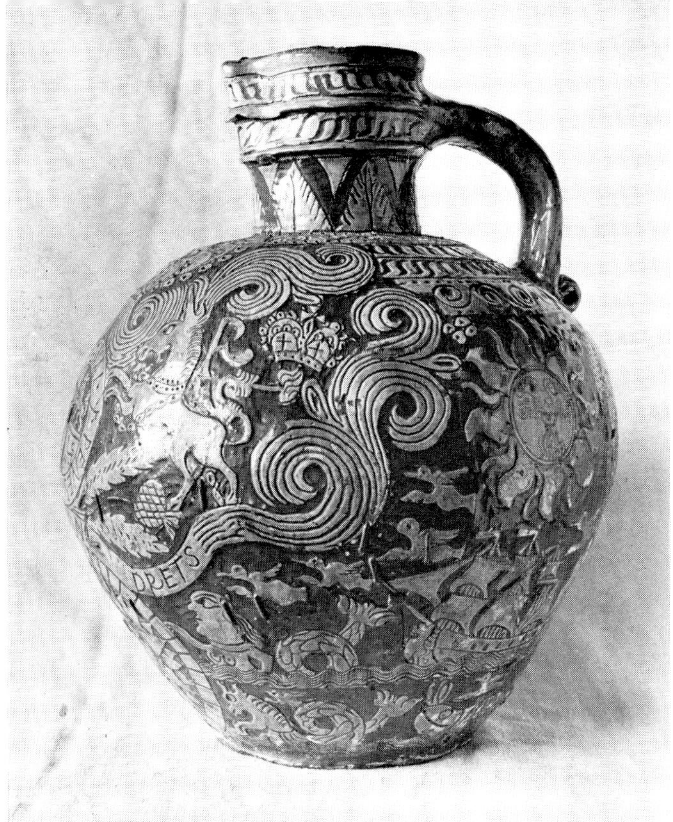


*Page 89* North Devon harvest jugs, showing the styles employed by John Hoyle of Bideford in 1860 (*left*) and by John Phillips of the same town in 1760 (*right*) (see notes on page 183)

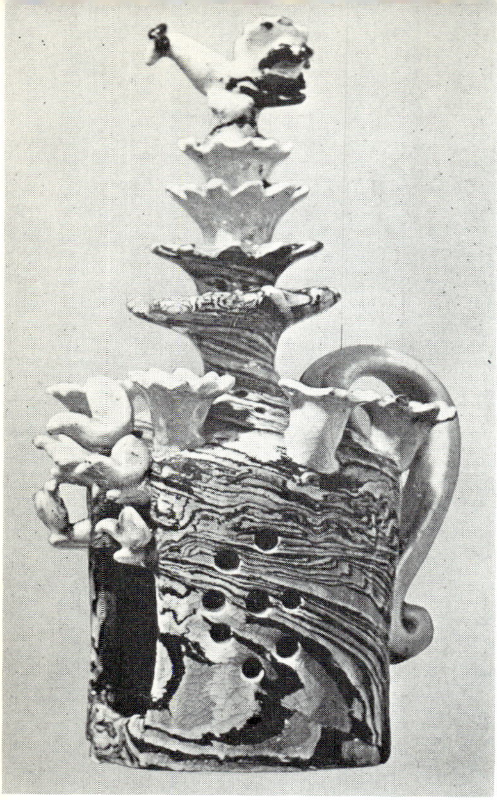

*Page 90* An exceptional lantern/candlestick made by John Kitchin of Whitehaven in the 1850s (*left*) and a pair of Halifax flower pot holders of the 1870s (*below*) (see notes on page 183)

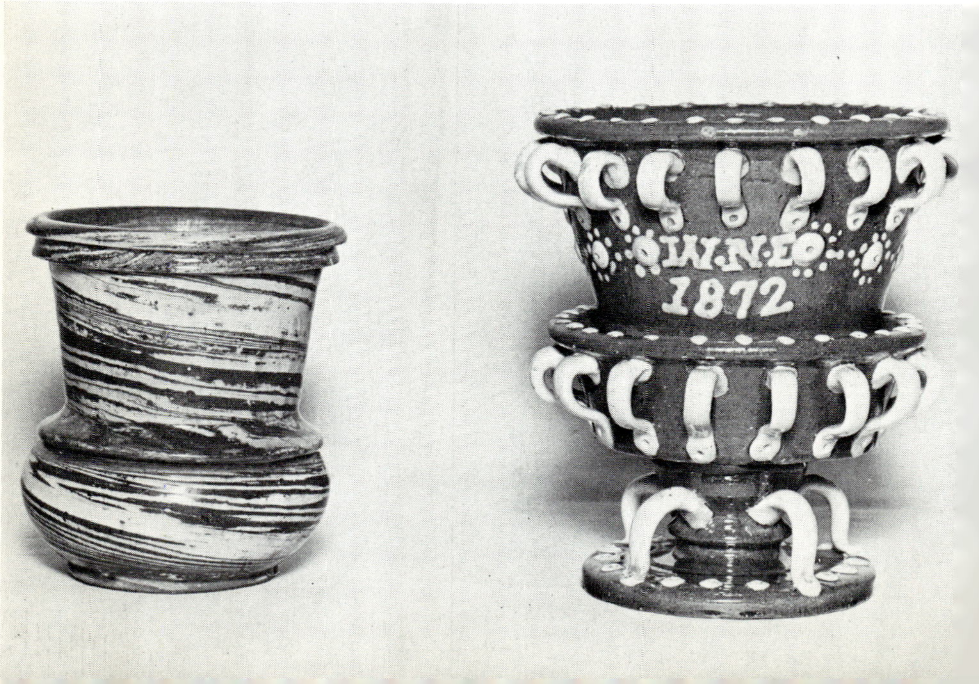

the vertical surfaces pressed back on four sides to give the pots a rectangular plan. As with other Halifax wares of this period, the decoration was always executed in a fairly liquid white slip. Such features as parallel horizontal slip bands or dates and initials were trailed on rapidly with great confidence and fluidity of movement, a strong contrast to the rather laboured neatness found on the later Halifax pieces. A fine specimen of this type is now in the Weston Park Museum, Sheffield (no. K 1937–23), its front and rear faces both having the initials 'A B' trailed with the date, 1798.

## *Wassail Cups*

In the apple-growing counties of Devon, Somerset, and, to a lesser degree, Sussex, the practice of wassailing the trees to make sure of a high yield was a fairly commonplace occurrence. In Somerset in particular on

> old Christmas Eve (5 January) or the eve of the Epiphany, it was the custom not long since . . . for the farmer with his men, to go out into the orchard, and to place toast steeped in cider, along with a jug of the liquor, up in the 'vork' of the biggest apple tree, by way of a libation; then all say:
>
> 'Apple tree, apple tree, I wassaail thee!
> To blow and to bear,
> Hat vulls, cap vulls, dree-bushell-bag-vulls!
> And my pockets vull too!
> Hip! Hip! Hooraw!' (bang with one or more guns)
>
> This ceremony and formula is repeated several times at different trees, with fresh firing of guns.[2]

As might be expected, the ceremony provided a good opportunity for holding a mid-winter celebration of which cider, ale, and good songs would constitute the chief ingredients. Ample evidence for this is given in the wassail cups made in north Devon early last century. The most interesting of these are undoubtedly the ones made at Fremington by Edmund Fishley. Measuring about 9in in height, these pots have bodies of approximately cylindrical outline, with two handles, a low domed lid and a front spout from which the liquid might be sucked. Their chief interest lies in their modelling. One of his pots in the Bideford Library Museum is decorated with four pairs of high-relief figures in eighteenth-century costume, the men wearing wigs, tricorn hats and frock coats, while the women have shawls and long dresses. On the lid sits a fiddler and a cat, the latter probably indicating the potter's views on the former's playing, the following lines being cut through the white slip beneath them:

> Give us the White Cockhade/Fiddler Bob and
> Come sit a down and merry be
> And think, my Master, comfort be.
> Ed. Fishley Maker Fremington Pottery
> Dec 16th 1843.

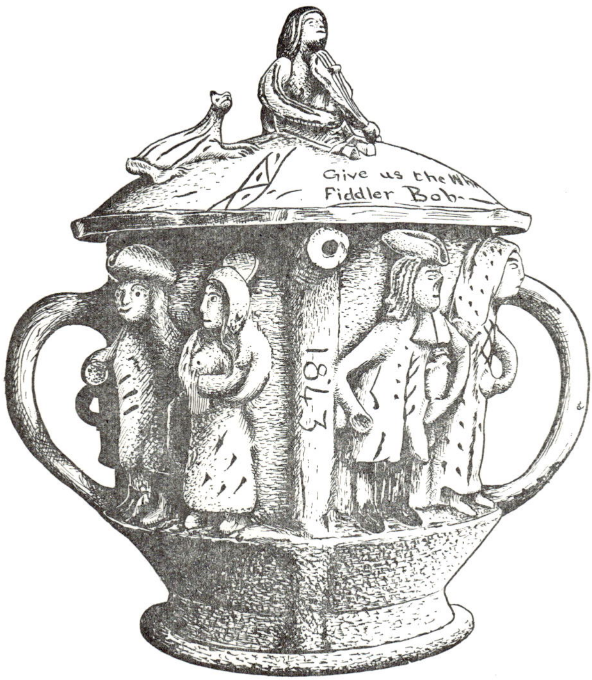


Fig 9 Wassail cup made by Edwin Fishley of Fremington in 1843

The presence of 'Fiddler Bob' to play such a rousing song as the 'White Cockade', coupled with the date of manufacture, leaves no doubt that wassailing the apple trees in north Devon was by no means a sober ceremony, the wassail cup being refilled on numerous occasions throughout the course of the evening.

*Notes for this chapter are on page 178*

## *Chapter Five*

# *Flower Pots*

The use of earthenware vessels for the growth and display of flowers is of considerable antiquity, having provided an important source of the country potter's trade since the mid-sixteenth century at least. At first specially made flower pots appear to have been made almost exclusively for the wealthier households which possessed large formal gardens. At Ingatestone Hall in Essex Sir William Petre was ordering '4 Pots for flowers' from Prentice, the potter of Stock, as early as 1550.[1] These would probably be quite ornamental in character, judging from other flower pots which have survived from this period. One fine group from the palatial Basing House near Basingstoke takes the form of a number of cylindrical and urn-shaped terracotta vases, the former being decorated with incised foliage designs, while the latter also bear the arms, crest and motto of their owner, the Marquess of Winchester.[2]

During the seventeenth century the use of flower pots became much more common in England, most gardening books assuming a plentiful supply of them in their instructions. 'Pot that earth, and set in it stock-gilly-flowers or wall-flowers,' advises Bacon in his *Sylva* of 1626, while Markham's *English Housewife* published in 1660 suggests: 'If you will set forth yellow flowers, take the pots of Primroses and Cowslips.' By the opening of the succeeding century flower pots were being made in the majority of the smaller potteries scattered throughout the country, but their quality varied considerably from one area to another. The major centres such as Stoke-on-

Trent or Ticknall could produce first-rate pots, but many of the smaller potteries could make only inferior wares. That at Potterspury in Northamptonshire was notorious, its 'garden pots [being] very apt to scale, and be broken in pieces by foul weather and frosts', according to John Morton's *Natural History of Northamptonshire*, published in 1712. The Potterspury pot-sellers told their customers that this defect could be cured by soaking the flower pots in oil, but as Morton continued, 'others who made that experiment have found it fail them'. The breakage of flower pots through frost must have been quite an expensive business, for in comparison to today's values they were by no means cheap. The account books of the Cornishman William Borlase[3] contain such entries as 'paid the potter for flowerpots etc. in full 5/6d', for 1739, and 'for 2 dozen flower pots 4/6d' for 1754, the latter entry giving a price of 2¼d per pot, quite a high price at this period for such a commonplace piece of garden equipment.

As with most other forms of coarse pottery, the flower pot was made in increasingly large numbers during the expansion of the urban potteries from the mid-eighteenth century. Besides being used for horticultural or botanical purposes either in large gardens or in specialised nurseries, it also became a semi-ornamental item in the home of the working man. As such it was an object in which pride was taken, the pot often being decorated in the local tradition with suitable flourishes such as flowers, fruits or leaves, together with the name of its owner, his village and the date. A good early example of this type can be seen in the museum of the Royal Cornish Institution at Truro. Decorated in the sgraffito technique, it is inscribed 'John C. D. Jenkins's Flower pot March 4 1826' 'John Tresise Potter Penzance 1826', these lines being separated by a male bust, probably representing Mr Jenkins, and two simple flower pots in outline. Through the efforts of the Mechanics' Institutes, the various church lecture societies and numerous national and local exhibitions of art and industry, aided by the proliferation of cheap but informative illustrated books, the public was encouraged to pursue an active interest in natural history topics from the 1830s onwards. This spate of public education had a great effect on the pottery trade for it popularised an interest in flowers as objects for study and as sources of colour and decoration within the home. If geraniums were required for the window sill, cut flowers or aspidistras for the parlour or rare ferns for the conservatory, it was necessary to provide them with a strong watertight container which only the potter could supply. Thus from the second quarter of the century onwards the country potter made an ever-increasing variety of flower pots to meet this growing demand. Initially the pots for household use were all decorated in the traditional manner of their own particular regions, but by the 1850s an almost universal technique of producing 'rustic wares' had been adopted in most potteries. This normally consisted of making the wares in a common red-firing fabric, the surface of which was scratched with a fork to give a bark-like finish. For additional reality clay 'knots' were frequently applied, each being tipped with a coating of white slip. For many potteries rustic ware became the most important single class of pottery made, one which provided the potters with a considerable source of pride. The Watsons of Wattisfield Pottery in Suffolk, for example, were pleased to call themselves 'Manufacturers of the famous TERRA-COTTA RUSTIC WARE', advising that 'Lovers of anything pretty and artistic for ferns should write for specimens'. The Harrises' pottery at Farnham in Surrey, meanwhile, produced a standard range of rustic wares, including the following green-glazed items:

| | | | |
|---|---|---|---|
| Rustic Fern Pots | 1/3d | per | dozen |
| Green Urns | 2/12/0d | ,, | ,, |
| Baskets | 2/6d | ,, | ,, |
| Rustic Wall Pots | 3/9d | ,, | ,, |
| Rustic Epergnes | 9/0d | ,, | ,, |
| Green Flower Stands | 18/0d | ,, | ,, |
| Bouquet Holders | 12/0d | ,, | ,, |

During the major development of the Arts and Crafts Movement from the 1880s onwards, numerous attempts were made by both amateur and professional artists to bring the country potter's wares up to a high aesthetic standard. In the production of 'art wares' designed exclusively for the decorative pottery market they achieved some quite effective results, but as far as flower pots and horticultural wares were concerned their efforts were not so successful. Early in 1890, for example, W. H. Allen, Art Master of Farnham School of Art, had produced a range of artistic designs for Absolom Harris's nearby pottery. Some of these, including the 'Rustic Fern Pots', sold well, but others were not at all popular, causing Absolom to complain that they 'were not suited to our customers, who wanted something to put flowers in'.

The production of highly ornamental flower pots continued to flourish up to the outbreak of World War I, but from that time on it fell into a rapid decline as plainer and more functional designs began to enjoy a much greater demand. Since then, the production of simple redware flower pots has been the mainstay of the industry, many gardeners still preferring their absorbent fabric to those of the smooth and waterproof plastic variety. Some ornamental horticultural wares have continued to be made since the 1920s, however, such as large garden vases, urns, jars and strawberry pots for use out of doors near porches and on terraces. All the existing country potteries continue to make these in large quantities.

Some of the most attractive flower pots to be made in the nineteenth century were those produced by George Fishley in the Fremington Pottery, north Devon. One of these, now in the possession of his great-great-great-grandson, is of the usual plant-pot shape, with a deep saucer round its base to receive any surplus water. Dating from *c*. 1800, it is decorated in a variety of ways, the motifs including thumbed strips round its rims, painted slip leaf-borders round its saucer and applied white leaf designs round its body, these being enriched by the addition of stamped berries, bunches of grapes and cupid masks to complete an extremely satisfying design. A rather plainer example, reputed to have been made by him *c*. 1810 (according to an old label) is now in the North Devon

Athenaeum at Barnstaple. This has the same tapering flower pot body and deep saucer, but is decorated with a simple border of ivy leaves executed in the resist technique just

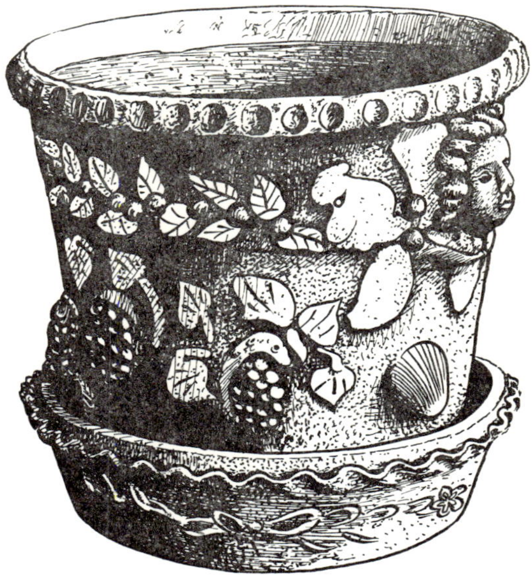

Fig 10 A flower pot by George Fishley of Fremington

below its rim. In his later years George Fishley concentrated on the production of small highly decorated pieces, including a number of wall pockets which were probably hung on internal walls to support small posies of flowers. A few pieces of this type are to be seen in the Royal Albert Museum at Exeter (no. 89/1928/3) and in the Fitzwilliam Museum at Cambridge (Glaisher Collection no. 91). Each pot measures 6in in height and takes the form of a conical vessel squeezed to an elongated plan to fit closely against the wall on which it hung. Across the top each pot has three full-sized figs applied in the typical golden-brown Fremington fabric, while their front faces are decorated still further with leaves, stars and round masks applied in white clay. Unfortunately none of the later north Devon potters produced work of this quality, the high standards of the eighteenth and early nineteenth centuries declining rapidly from the 1850s onwards. Some of the jardinières made in the early twentieth century by such potters as James Radcliffe were particularly hideous, their florid sgraffito chrysanthemum patterns and scalloped knife-cut rims showing little evidence of either good craftsmanship or acceptable aesthetic standards.

In Sussex the most interesting flower pots and rustic wares were almost certainly those made at the Mitchell's pottery in Rye. Evidence for their early participation in this field is provided by the flower pots and stands probably made by William Mitchell. One inscribed 'RYE POTTERY AUG. 19.1840' is known from Hastings, while another bearing a bricks and mortar pattern in the British Museum (no. Q2) has the words 'Rye (Sussex) Pottery' incised across its base. It was William's younger son, Frederick, who started to produce decorative wares at the pottery from the 1850s, however. By making his own moulds of fired clay, he was able to press out ornamental details such as oak leaves, chrysanthemums, hops, buttercups or doves from clay previously stained with coloured metallic oxides. These could then be applied to the ware, which was subsequently fired and glazed to bring out their colours. When the Hastings and St Leonard's Industrial Exhibition was held in September 1867, 'Mr Frederick Mitchell, Cadboro' Pottery, Rye' was awarded a bronze medal as winner of the first prize for Sussex pottery. Thus encouraged, he leased a site in Rye on which to build the Belle Vue Pottery where, from 1868 to his death in 1875, he specialised in the production of decorative rustic wares, including many types of ornamental flower pots and jardinières. The pottery was continued after his death by his widow, assisted by his nephew, Frederick Thomas Mitchell (1864–1920).

In the remainder of the south and midlands very few potters attempted works of such complexity; instead they restricted themselves to relatively plain rustic wares. Typical of these were the products of George Franklin of the Leafield Pottery in Oxfordshire. These consisted mainly of unglazed terracotta flower pots, bowls and wall pots, examples of which are to be seen in the Oxford City and County Museum at Fletcher's House, Woodstock (for instance, no. 1733). In a few of the larger and more enterprising works pressed-ware garden urns were also made to order. These were made from large two- or three-piece moulds of either plaster of Paris or unglazed earthenware, thick slabs of clay being beaten into them to form sections which were then united to form a complete vessel. Fishley Holland has recorded how an old sock filled with rags would be used as an effective beater for this purpose at Fremington, while a number of other craftsmen, such as Messrs A. and R. Harris of Farnham and Mr Richard Bateson of Burton-in-Lonsdale, can remember similar techniques being employed at their own potteries.

Further north, a few potteries made flower pots in fairly characteristic shapes which enable them to be identified with relative ease. The Shelton Pottery, near Lancaster, for example, made a speciality of short, round red-bodied pots which were topped by a semi-circular strap of clay which passed diametrically over the mouth of the vessel to form a handle. These were chiefly made in the latter half of the nineteenth century, and may be distinguished by their crude workmanship and even cruder white slip-trailing, such inscriptions as 'a present from Shelton' being typical. The Lancaster Museum possesses one of these, which appears to be the only one in a public collection.

An ancestor of Richard Bateson of the Burton-in-Lonsdale potteries was trained at Shelton and was apparently responsible for the introduction of the above form of flower pot into the Burton repertoire. Instead of being allowed to remain in its coarse and imperfect form, however, it was quickly modified by the potters to become quite an attractive and highly saleable piece. This is amply shown by two examples in the Yorkshire Museum at York (nos. 92/a, 92/b), these being made at the Town End Pottery, Burton-in-Lonsdale, in about 1870. The body, instead of being short and round in outline, was brought to a vase-shaped silhouette, while instead of having a row of open drainage holes round its base it was now given a deep encircling saucer thrown as one of its integral features. The handle, too, was completely remodelled, now being formed as a twisted cable of red and white rolls of clay decorated with applied white pellets. The slip-trailing, glazing or plain red or agate-ware fabrics were also improved, so that the products of the two potteries are now immediately distinguishable, though they still have the same basic form.

Deeper into Yorkshire, in the Halifax area, the problem of identifying pottery with a particular works is rendered rather more complicated by the fact that a number of potters moved fairly frequently from one pottery to another within the group, making almost identical wares wherever they went. This is typified by the well-documented career of Nicholas Taylor,[4] one of the most interesting and versatile of the Halifax potters. His wares are of an unusually high standard, and so it is possible to identify them with a fair degree of accuracy, although unless there is some form of internal documentation, it is impossible to state at which of his numerous places of work they were made. In 1938 his widow presented a collection of his wares to the Halifax Museums, where they may now be seen. They include such items as one of the rustic-ware flower baskets he made at Castleford in 1914 (no. 1938/5.2). This has a shallow oval base of red clay, rusticated on its outer surfaces but with an internal coating of white slip on which are scattered a number of transfer-printed bouquets of coloured flowers. Arching over the base, from one side of the scalloped and gold-lustred rim to the other, is a handle of entwined rusticated rods, these being well supplied with beautifully modelled pink roses in three dimensions. The use of such industrial techniques as transfer-printing and metallic oxides to give pinks, blues or other non-traditional colours is quite unusual in country pottery, but at this particular period the potters were still trying to 'improve' their wares to compete with the factory-made products. With this in mind he next developed his 'Nicholas Ware' at the Ogden Pottery, typical pieces in the Halifax collection (nos. 1938.5/9 and 10) showing this to have been a range of flower vases and plates covered in a surface marbling of white, blue and pink slips.

In contrast to the 'improved' wares pioneered by Nicholas Taylor were the thoroughly straightforward pots made by Samuel Catherall, who worked at the Soil Hill Pottery, Halifax from about 1830 to within a short while of his death in about 1887. A well-provenanced example of his ornamental flower pots in the Yorkshire Museum (no. 88/a–99/d) takes the form of a tall flower pot mounted on a pedestal base similar to that shown on page 90. Beneath the rims of both the pot and its base are twenty miniature handles applied as ornaments in white clay, while round the pot alone, just below the handles, is a slip-trailed border of rings and dots, these being a favourite motif on many of his wares (see p 17). Between the border and the handles runs the following incised inscription, which establishes its origins conclusively: 'S.C. born March 19th, 1807 and made this pot April 29, 1865, at Swilling End.' Samuel Catherall also made a variety of flower pots decorated with applied white clay pellets overstamped with face-mask, leaf or shell designs, two such pots in the Yorkshire Museum collection (nos. 87/b and 87/c) bearing these motifs in conjunction with such simple slip-trailed inscriptions as 'L.P.B.1877' and '1877'; the latter is surrounded by a small rectangular cartouche of slip dots. It is likely that the Catheralls, or their successors at Soil Hill, the Buttons, also made rustic-ware flower pots with the usual rough-combed surfaces and applied knots, for a number of the farmers living near the pottery still use wares of this type, which they say were purchased there in the late nineteenth century.

The Mortons of Sallendine Nook, the most southerly of the Halifax group, also made rustic wares, these being either pots with white slipped knots, or else 'log baskets' which consisted of twelve small 'logs' of red clay built up to form an open-framed container some six inches square (eg, Yorks.Mus.89/a and 90/a). A number of other Halifax potteries, such as those at Howcans and Small Clues also made ornamental flower pots, but their decoration was usually quite plain, consisting of either agate-ware fabrics, simple slip-trailed designs, or zig-zag knife cutting around the rims.

The last potter to produce hand-thrown flower pots in Yorkshire was Mr George Curtis of Littlethorpe Pottery, near Ripon. Unlike those of Halifax, the wares of Littlethorpe were almost entirely without ornament, though they occasionally reached immense sizes. One of Mr Curtis's instructors at the pottery, Albert Kitson, specialised in such vessels, his lyd-high tree pots made for the nearby Newby Hall gardens being some of the largest pots to be thrown in England. Following in the Littlethorpe tradition, Mr Curtis continued to produce 'bigwares' up to the early 1970s, adopting many forms of unglazed terracotta wall pots, terrace jars and strawberry pots to keep pace with the rapidly changing fashions of the last half century.

In addition to flower pots and vases the country potters also made a number of curious items for use with animals, birds, and insects in the garden. One of these was the nineteenth-century mole-trap (see figure 11 on p 104). This was a deep pot, almost 1ft high, which was pierced by a small hole half-way down one side. The pot was filled with water up to the level of the hole, a hollow wooden box was placed over its mouth and, thus primed, the whole trap was set in position on the line of a mole's intended run. As the mole passed through the central section of the box a trap-door precipitated it down into the water below, the spring returning the trap-door to its original position in preparation for the next mole.

At the other side of the country, in East Anglia, a new variety of pot was introduced from the Netherlands in the late sixteenth century. This was the sparrow pot, first seen built into the thatch of houses in the paintings of the Breughels, but used beneath the eaves in England into at least the late nineteenth century. In form the pot resembled a large jar with a wide shallow rim extending around its neck.

Through this, and down into the body of the pot, a hole was pierced to receive a short twig on which the sparrows might perch when nesting inside. These pots were not installed for ornithological interest but were used to provide a supply

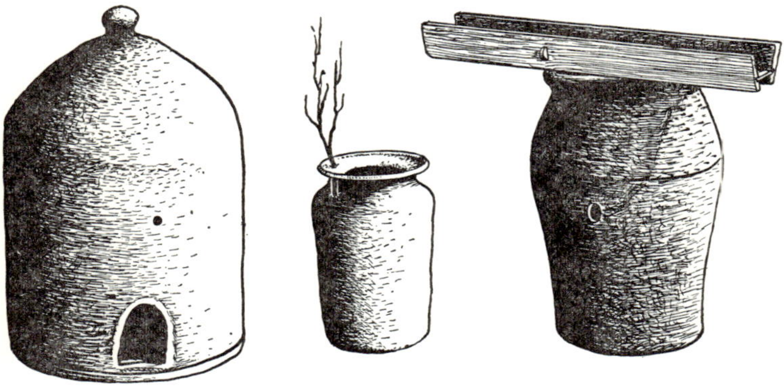

Fig 11 A bee super, sparrow pot and mole trap of nineteenth-century date

of sparrows. For an East Anglican farm worker these could provide an additional source of income, since many parishes offered up to fourpence a dozen for the sparrows, which inflicted considerable damage to the crops. They could also provide a source of food, for when all other meats were prohibitively expensive the sparrow was both legal to trap and easy to catch.[5]

Honey could also be used as additional food for the table and the potter was sometimes called upon to provide a ceramic hive. These appear to have been made most frequently in eighteenth-century Cornwall where, in 1743, William Borlase 'paid the potter for four clome beehives', though he had also purchased a number in the previous year.[6] The bee super, another useful product of the country potter, was mainly used in upper Wensleydale in Yorkshire; it was probably a speciality of the nineteenth-century Redmire Pottery near Castle Bolton. An example from Askrigg, a Wensleydale village, is now in the Bradford City Museum collection. It is in the form of a tall bottle with a closed top and an open base, and was placed over the top of a cylindrical straw bee-skep to act as a honey storage chamber for the bees, the combs being removed quite easily from its interior when required.

*Notes for this chapter are on page 178.*

## *Chapter Six*

# *Jokes and Puzzles*

Puzzle cups and jugs have made a most interesting section of the country potter's trade for a considerable period. Probably the earliest English puzzle jug in existence was excavated from the Angel Inn, Oxford, where it had probably been in use some six hundred years ago. Even at this early date the jug (British Museum no. 86) shows various features which have formed a basis for many of the later examples, including false bottoms and the use of a hollow handle by which the liquid might be sucked up through a sucking spout at the rim. The puzzle jug was still in its infancy, however, and it was not until the late sixteenth century that it apparently reached a mature stage of development. This is demonstrated by a group in the national collections dated between 1569 and 1571.[1] Each of these jugs has an ovoid body supporting an almost cylindrical neck and a broad, round-sectioned rim. The section about the neck is pierced by a number of cross-shaped perforations which make it impossible to pour from the spout without spilling most of the contents. To use these jugs, therefore, the liquid has to be sucked up through the tubular handle, round the hollow rim and up a short mouth-piece which projects forwards in the normal position for a spout. The authenticity of these jugs is rather suspect, for it is extremely unusual for Elizabethan coarse pottery to bear a definite date. Their materials, too, consisting of a coarse red fabric covered with a white slip and an unusually well-worn olive-green glaze, tend to suggest that they might just as well be the products of a nineteenth-century faker.

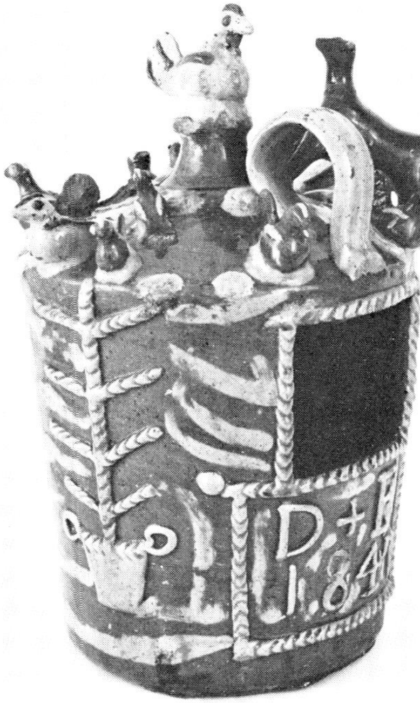

*Page 107* Salt kits, the applied details of the 1847 example by the Kitsons of Woodman House, Halifax (*left*) contrasting with the confident slip-trailing seen on the 1887 kit by the Schofields of Weatheriggs, near Penrith (*below*) (see notes on pages 183–4)

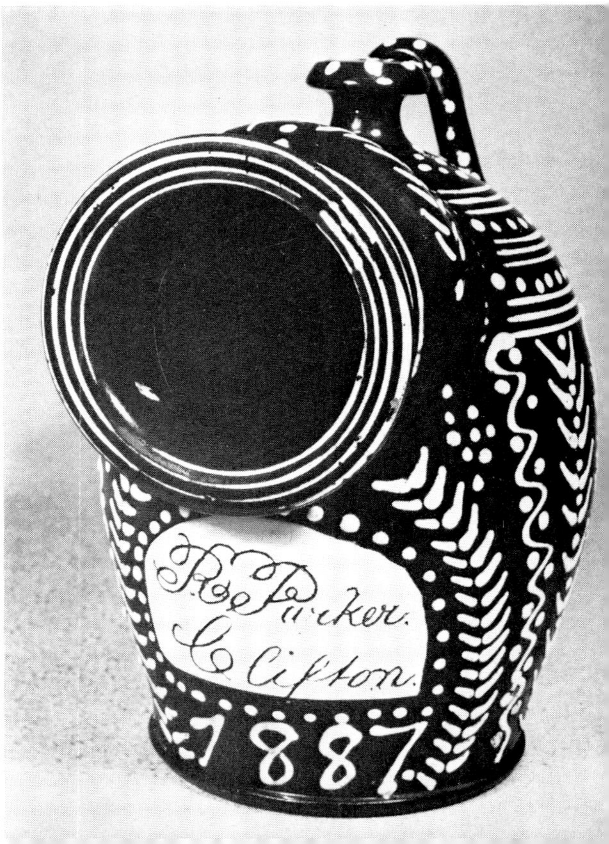

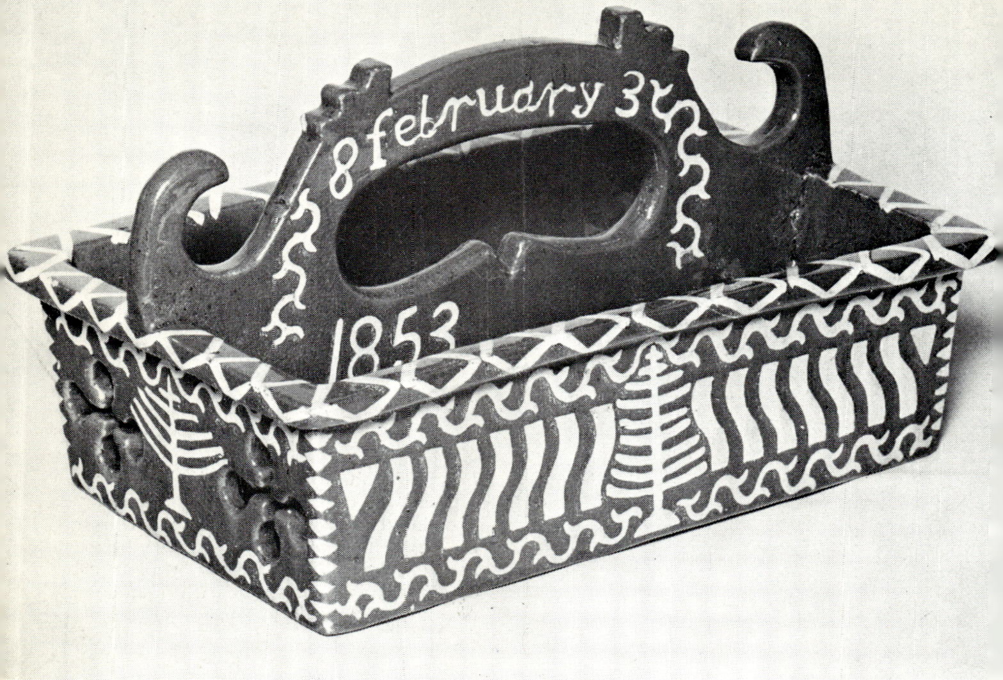


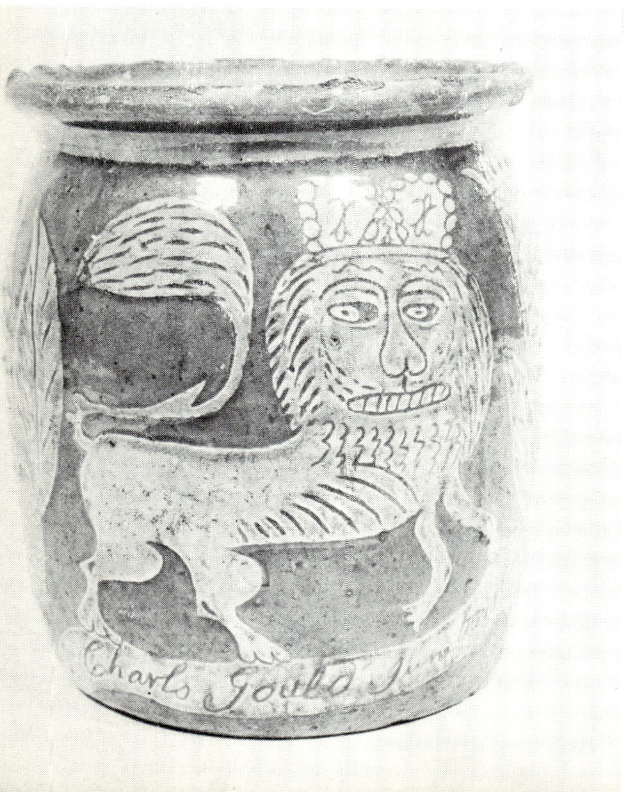


*Page 108* The style of the lion seen on the honey pot (*left*) confirms John Bird of Bideford as its maker, just as that of the cutlery box (*above*) is evidence for its being made at Howcans, Halifax (see notes on page 184)

It is certain that puzzle jugs of an outstanding quality were being made in a number of potteries during the seventeenth century. At Wrotham, for example, the potters were making short, round-bodied jugs enriched with large slip-trailed initials and dates and free-standing figures of animals and men along their rims (eg, British Museum no. D11). Staffordshire was producing jugs of the more usual shape, but with heart-shaped perforations, bird sucking-spouts and snake-entwined handles (eg, British Museum no. D83), while at Yearsley in north Yorkshire John Wedgwood was incising his name across the fronts of his plainer northern greenware pieces. The real popularity of the puzzle jug was yet to come, however, and it was with the eighteenth-century expansion of the craft that these trick jugs came into their own.

Probably the first potteries to produce decorated puzzle jugs in fairly large numbers were those at Donyatt in Somerset, numerous examples of their wares surviving from the 1740s onwards. With their rather tall bulbous bodies, slightly constricted cylindrical necks and broad rolled rims they followed the shape of the earlier puzzle jugs fairly closely. Even when most other potters started to add extra mouthpieces and pierced finger-holes to make their jugs more difficult to use, the Donyatt men still continued to apply a single sucking-spout which projected almost 1in above the front of the jug's rim, just opposite the topmost joint of the handles. This early shape, combined with the typical red Donyatt fabric covered in its white slip and green-flecked yellow lead glaze, remained fairly uniform throughout the life of these potteries, but minor variations in either the piercing of the neck or the choice of the rhyme enable the earlier ones to be distinguished from those of a later period with a moderate degree of certainty. One of the earliest dated Donyatt puzzle jugs is in the Hollings Collection at Temple Newsam House, near Leeds (see p 53). This has a series of crosses and small circles pierced through its wall round the neck and bears the following inscription: 'Fill me full Drink of Me while you woul/ Mary Roge 1740', in sgraffito across the front of its body; a number of rosettes and tulip motifs decorate the areas to the left and right. In the Glaisher Collection at Cambridge are two very similar Donyatt jugs (nos. 164 and 171) which have the same form of piercing, decoration and rhyme, these being dated 1749 and 1799 respectively. As the eighteenth century progressed, however, there was a tendency to use rather longer and more interesting inscriptions, while the cross-shaped piercing was slowly replaced by circular holes, even though the former was occasionally used as late as the 1820s. Typical Donyatt rhymes express such sentiments as:

> When this you see pray think on mee 1777[2]
>
> Fill me up with Liker that is sweet for it is good When Friends do met 1792[3]
>
> Come Drink of Me and Merry Be. R. Madeck Esq. Sept 5 1834[4]
>
> Fill me up to the brim and give a tip to a friend Come Drink of me and merry be my Friends. Robert Nappee Wrantage Somerset May 17th 1853[5]
>
> The Rose is Reed ye Leaf is Green ye Days are Past That we have Seen 1791 IC BC SW.[6]

Up to the early nineteenth century these wares were rarely signed by the potters themselves, but slowly potters adopted the habit of inscribing their names beneath their more elaborate products. In 1816, for example, a puzzle jug[7] bearing the verses

> When this you
> See pray think on
> Mee and Bear it in
> your mind for i am sill
> times at your house
> Speak By me as you find
>
> except this geft
> my dear from mee

was signed by the potter 'Isaac Trott Donyatt near Ilminster', while from the 1860s James Rogers impressed the stamp 'ROGERS & SONS CROCK STRETT POTTERY'[8] beneath many of his finer pieces.

Puzzle jugs of a particularly distinctive pattern were also produced at Bridgwater in Somerset during the latter years of the nineteenth century. These were the work of J. Nicholls, a craftsman employed at the pottery of J. Brown & Sons for forty years up to his death in 1908. Unlike the Donyatt pieces, his wares were made entirely from the local warm red-firing clay, no trailed or dipped slips being used at all. Instead, his decorative motifs took the form of applied sprig-moulded details pressed out from the same fabric as the pots themselves. One of his few recorded pieces is now in the Glaisher Collection at Cambridge (no. 181, see p 54). This has the bulbous body and rolled rim seen on most puzzle jugs, but in addition it also has the unique characteristic of three sucking spouts rising vertically above its rim instead of the normal one. Besides these, the neck is pierced by numerous circular punched holes, while the body itself bears a stag-hunting scene, with mounted huntsmen, hounds and a stag applied in low relief over an area of dot-textured 'grass'. His mark 'J. Nicholls' impressed in a palace-script typeface is to be seen across the front of the pot, just beneath the central mouthpiece.

In north Devon puzzle jugs were infrequently made and, since the earliest extant examples appear to date from the 1780s, it is likely that they were copied from those of the Donyatt potteries, which had been in production at least forty years before. The earlier north Devon puzzle jugs were almost identical to those of Donyatt, but had vertical slots separated by rows of dots spaced round their necks instead of the pierced crosses found at Donyatt. In addition the north Devon potters retained their own styles of sgraffito decoration, as might have been expected. A typical early piece was illustrated in the *Connoisseur* in 1915.[9] It had been discovered while the bottom of a well at Skelford, Devon, was being cleaned out and it has the inscription 'Pray drink your fill, but do not spill, for I shall take it very ill/June ye 16,1789' incised round the widest section of its squat body, while above and below run borders of running scroll and zig-zag patterns respectively. An almost identical jug in the Glaisher Collection (no. 116), probably made in the same pottery, invites the drinker thus: 'Pray Fill me up with Good Strong Beer Then Suck it out and never fear 1790.' Also in the Glaisher Collection are two slightly different north Devon puzzle jugs (nos. 166 and 65). One has four sucking spouts and both circular holes and sloping slots cut through its neck. It reads:

Fill me with Ale with wine or water
Any of the 3 it makes No matter
Drink me Dry if you are willing
In doing so you'l win a shilling

William Courtic February 1 1791 JP.

It has been suggested that the final initials are those of John Pidler, who worked at the Fremington Pottery early last century. Certainly this is likely to be so, for one Mary Courtice, probably a relation of the above William, had a jug made at Fremington by Edmund Fishley in 1824 (see p 78). The other jug, this time with three sucking spouts and piercings forming the name 'John Arnold' is dated to November 13th, 1827. Its inscription reads: 'drink to mee with your Heart and fill unto the mark then drink mee pray without spilling or you will [pay] thre shiling', indicating that bets might be taken on the drinker's ability to solve the puzzle and suck up his ale.

The later north Devon puzzle jugs were chiefly made by Edwin Beer Fishley of Fremington, most of them being conscious imitations of earlier pieces. The Royal Albert Memorial Museum at Exeter has one which bears his signature, this probably being made about the turn of the century. Its red fabric is covered in a white slip, through which is cut the following verse:

Within this jug there is good liquor
Fit for Parson or for Vicar
But how to drink and not to spill
Will try the utmost of yr. skill.

Finally this jug was given an overall coating of a rich and glossy green glaze, this being a particularly suitable finish for one of his reproduction 'medieval' wares. A much more interesting jug, almost certainly made by Edwin Fishley, is now in the Yorkshire Museum at York (no. 69/a). For some time this piece has raised considerable problems for the ceramic historian, for its details are unusual, to say the least. While following the normal puzzle jug form with swelling body and cylindrical neck, it also shows a remarkable variety of influences. The rim itself was brought up above the horizontal rim-tube, for example, and knife-cut in imitation of eighteenth-century Nottingham salt-glazed stoneware puzzle jugs; the piercing was of the vertical slot and circular hole pattern so characteristic of north Devon; the impressed initials were identical to those on seventeenth-century Wrotham tygs, while the mouthpieces or sucking spouts were formed as serpents' heads, their bodies extending in coils down the pot's sides to copy those found by Dr Schliemann in ancient Troy and Mycenae. This extraordinary ceramic amalgam began to make sense only when a greater knowledge of Edwin Fishley had been acquired. It is now known that his patrons took him up to the London museums to see the more important ceramic collections; Mr J. Phillips took him to see Schliemann's exhibition, for example. As a result he took to copying Japanese, Russian, Trojan, Mycenaean and classical Greek wares, and also specialised in the production of reproduction English wares, Wrotham providing many of his favourite models. This knowledge, reinforced by the jug's north Devon fabric, at once made it clear that Edwin Fishley was the only man who could possibly have made this vessel, and wares of this type can now be attributed to him with a high degree of confidence.

Such composite and over-stylised jugs were almost certainly unique to Fremington; in Yorkshire and Lancashire, where many nineteenth-century examples were made, the potters preferred to continue developing within their own local traditions. It is quite difficult to distinguish between the products of these two northern counties, for their materials are quite similar, and comparatively few well-provenanced pieces are known. There are some minor differences in overall shape, as the Lancashire jugs tend to have rather longer necks and shorter bodies than are seen on those from Yorkshire. Slight differences in decorative technique may also be noted. At the Cliviger pottery in the eastern Lancashire Pennines the potters applied bold pads of clay round the bodies of their jugs, rolling an ornamental butter-marker over them to produce an attractive pattern of leaves and thistles. One jug of this type used to be housed in the Borough Museum at Todmorden, a collection which has now been totally dispersed. This impressive piece had three spouts and piercing, and bore the inscription ' WBLB JAN 19.1844' inlaid in white clay round its red body. A further puzzle jug made in one of the east Lancashire potteries is now in the collection at Rufford Old Hall near Ormskirk. Dated 1865, it has a tall cylindrical neck pierced round its upper and lower edges with borders of alternate flat-bottomed and inverted triangles to give a simple trellis effect, while about its body the name of its original owner, 'Edward Dalton Croston', is trailed in white slip.

At the other side of the Pennines, in west Yorkshire, a number of fairly well-provenanced jugs is known, but here an important lesson may be learned, for research has shown that some well-known pieces have been considerably misdated by their former owners. When Oxley Grabham, a former curator of the Yorkshire Museum, was building up his great ceramics collection in the opening decades of the twentieth century, he visited every available source of old Yorkshire pottery, including working potters, old pottery sites, market stalls and shops. Wherever he managed to acquire a piece he made careful inquiries to establish when and where it had been made, noting this information either in the museum's catalogue or on a label attached to the pot itself. In this way he collected two puzzle jugs made at the Howcans pottery, Halifax, these being dated 1842 and 1883, and one made at 'Denholme, 1857'. Recent examination of these pieces in the light

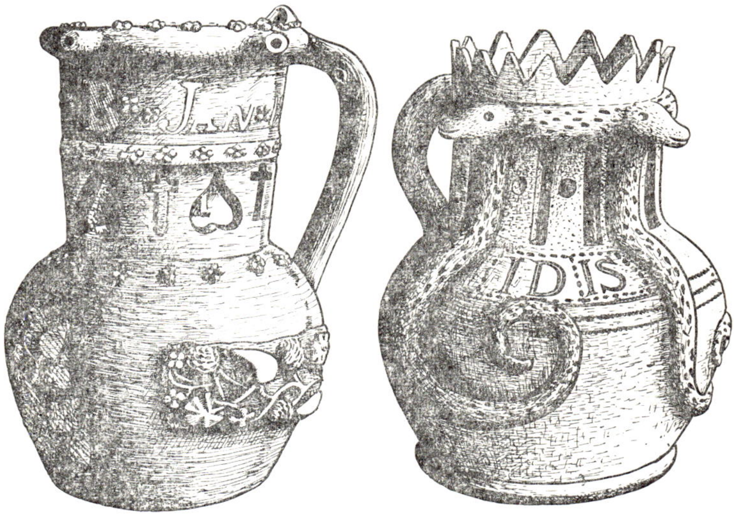


Fig 12 Puzzle jugs made in the traditional manner at the Cliviger Pottery, Lancashire, in 1844 (left), and in the Wrotham–north Devon–Nottingham–Trojan style adopted by E. B. Fishley of Fremington in the late nineteenth century (right)

of increased knowledge and experience has proved that they are not quite what they seem. The two 'Howcans' jugs are in fact from Burton-in-Lonsdale, their materials, techniques and designs being totally different from those of any Halifax pottery. The Denholme piece, meanwhile, dated by Oxley Grabham's informant to 1857, bears the signature of 'Nicholas Taylor, Denholme'; but as Mr Taylor was not born until 1868 and did not commence potting at Denholme until the 1880s, this date is impossibly early.

The production of puzzle jugs appears to have begun in

west Yorkshire during the 1830s, the potters of Burton-in-Lonsdale making two distinct varieties from this date. The most common (for instance, Yorkshire Museum nos. 67/a and b, Burnap Collection no. B756) has a fairly tall ovoid body in a dark red fabric, its comparatively short cylindrical neck being pierced with small triangular perforations to give an open trellis-like appearance. There are usually five sucking spouts, in addition to which an air-hole is pierced through the underside of the handle, near the rim. Jugs of this type require a high degree of skill on the part of the drinker, for all the holes have to be sealed before a single drop of liquid can be sucked from them. As with all Burton-in-Lonsdale wares, the white slip decoration is always of a very high standard, rows of fine dots being trailed round the piercings of the neck, while the body invariably bears the following rhyme:

> Gentlemen now try your skill,
> Ill hold you Sixpence if you will,
> That you don't drink unless you spill.

The majority of these jugs are also dated, the years being trailed in white slip along the topmost curve of the handle. The second variety of puzzle jug was made by Richard Bateson (*c.* 1840) of the Waterside Pottery, Burton-in-Lonsdale. His jugs, often produced in a red and white agate-ware fabric, have S-shaped knife-cut perforations at the neck, six sucking spouts, a rather rough-surfaced angular handle, and the rhyme:

> GENTLEMEN DRINK
> & LET YOUR SKILL BE TESTED
> & A FORFEIT MADE
> IF ANYTHING
> BE WASTED

impressed across its front in a plain sans-serif typeface.

In the Halifax potteries the production of puzzle jugs probably began in the 1850s, for no examples dating to the early nineteenth century have yet been recorded. One of the first potters to make such wares here was Samuel Catherall of the Soil Hill Pottery. His jugs are always made in a rather plain and robust manner, usually having five white-tipped sucking spouts and piercing round their necks in the vertical slot and round hole pattern which undoubtedly originated in north Devon. Unlike other jugs with this type of piercing, Samuel's have their circular holes punched through small round pads of white clay to produce a unique decorative effect. Occasionally he also used simple slip-trailed designs to enrich his jugs, the most common taking the form of a single band of circles and dots as seen on his candle holder on p 17. On order-made pieces, meanwhile, he included both the date and the owner's initials. A good example of his work is now in the Shibden Hall Museum, Halifax (no. AH 391), inscribed 'G.W.1878'. The other major 'fineware' thrower of the Halifax area was Nicholas Taylor. His puzzle jugs, which are usually signed 'Nicholas Taylor, Denholme' across the base, follow no single pattern, for he was continually adopting new designs in an attempt to improve his wares. There may be three or four sucking spouts round the rim, these often being interspersed with additional air holes to render drinking more difficult, and the neck may be pierced with circular, cross-shaped, keyhole or star-shaped perforations. Often his wares are devoid of all ornament, but on some pieces either trailed or dipped white slip is used quite effectively. A signed jug of his in the Shibden Hall collection (no. 1950/60) has a bib of white slip dipped on to its front into which, in sgraffito, is cut the following: 'Puzzle/It's good when tha gets it' within a simple border of stylised tendrils. A number of other Halifax potters also made puzzle jugs, but their identities have not yet been established. Certainly they could achieve very high standards, however, as is seen in the unprovenanced wares found in various West Riding museums. One of the most interesting of these in the Halifax Museum's collection (no. AH2783) has the lower half of its red body dipped into white slip, the potter using this as a ground on which to cut in sgraffito the lines below;

> From 'Mother Earth' I claim my birth
> I'm made a joke for man
> But now I'm here filled with good cheer
> Come taste me if you can
>
> Harry D. Beanland
> Police Inspector
> Halifax Boro'

Puzzle jugs formed only part of the country potter's repertoire of tricks, for he also designed a great variety of cups and mugs which incorporated surprises or puzzles for the drinker. Even in the early seventeenth century, when tygs and posset pots were provided with quite obvious sucking spouts to enable their contents to be sucked from beneath a thick and glutinous froth, the potters had contrived to make some of the spouts solid, so that the unwary might suck long and hard without success.[10] By the late seventeenth and early eighteenth centuries the Staffordshire potters were making extremely fine puzzle or fuddling cups with six or seven semi-spherical cups mounted round the tubular rim of a deep ornamentally pierced bowl. At first sight it looked as if it would be impossible to drain one cup without spilling the contents of the remainder, but as each cup communicated with its neighbour by means of a hole cut through its base into the hollow rim beneath, a careful drinker could drain the whole vessel by steadily sipping from a single cup. Some examples also have two ornamental handles, the thumb-pieces of which conceal hidden mouthpieces. Later examples of this type are fairly plain, with six slightly bell-shaped cups mounted on a circular tube about 8in or 9in across by 1½in in diameter. From one side of this tube a tall curving mouthpiece rises to allow the drinker to suck up the contents of the whole vessel, its capacity being slightly over 1 quart. Most of these Staffordshire fuddling cups were made in a pale buff-firing clay glazed to a light-yellow colour with a transparent lead glaze, bold splashes of dark-brown manganese or iron-rich glazes giving them a particularly rich mottled finish. In exceptional cases, however, they were produced in a dark-red agate ware. One of these magnificent pieces was presented by Enoch Wood to the King of Saxony in 1835. This is now in the Staatliche Porzellansammlung in Dresden, where the accession book records the cup as 'No. 42, Drinking Vessel made for the purpose of exhibiting tricks in Legerdemain'.

Cups with numerous compartments were also made in the Donyatt potteries, but these followed rather simpler and earlier designs. Instead of having each compartment mounted individually on a base-ring, as in Staffordshire, the Donyatt potters stuck each small cup to its neighbour, a hole being pierced through each junction to allow the liquid to flow freely from one cup to another. Cups of this type were first made in the Lambeth delft-ware kilns of the mid-seventeenth century, but by the 1680s at least sgraffito-ware copies were being competently made at Donyatt, here being known as 'Jolly Boys' from one of the more common inscriptions they bore. The earliest of these vessels are formed as a triangle of three small cups, each being linked to its neighbour by a short twisted cable of clay, a plain example extending outwards from each of the three corners. As with all the finer Donyatt pieces, the red clay fabric was covered with a white slip and an overall pale-yellow lead glaze, the latter being flecked to a rich green colour here and there due to impurities of copper. Perhaps the oldest extant example is now in the Glaisher Collection (no. 161), bearing the date 1684 on each cup; but a second one in the Somerset County Museum at Taunton follows this fairly closely, having the inscription 'THREE MERY BOYS 1697' cut round it in sgraffito capitals. By the early eighteenth century 'Jolly Boys' with seven, eight or ten chambers were being made at Donyatt, each having such simple decorative motifs as tulips, inscriptions and dates freely scratched through their white slips. Some of these inscriptions were used at random, including lines such as 'BE MERY AND WISE 1702',[11] which was probably copied from a piece of metropolitan slipware, and others such as:

> When [this you see Pray] Think on me 1729 ES[12]
>
> Fill me full while you woul 1757[13]
>
> I love but you alone 1738 MW 1738[14]
>
> My frend is He That Love me will But Ho He is I cannot tall IM 1770[15]

Other inscriptions appear to have enjoyed considerable use at one period alone, being almost unknown before or after their single spate of popularity. In 1766, for example, the phrase 'Fill this Cup and Drink it up'[16] was in common use, while in the early 1770s allusions to the patron's intended as his 'delight' became more common, as in: '1770 No star so bright as my delight'[17] and 'In your sight is my delight.'[18] By the 1790s a more apologetic approach was being tried, with: 'The geft is small but good will is all GM JG 1792'.[19] But from the opening of the nineteenth century such long inscriptions were abandoned, brief lines such as 'Good Cider 1833',[20] being considered sufficient.

Care has to be taken in collecting these cups, for they were occasionally copied in the late nineteenth century. One in Stoke-on-Trent Museum's collection (no. 598 P44) has a number of strange features—the cups are not of the true Donyatt shape, the twisted handles are over-emphasised, the glaze is rather too thin, pale and bubbled, with green stains which are too bright, while the sgraffito inscription 'DRINK AND MERY 1693' is cut very stiffly instead of flowing naturally. The most disturbing feature, however, is the fabric, which shows the deep flesh colour typical of north Devon, thus suggesting that it is in fact another of Edwin Beer Fishley's less successful 'reproductions'.

# *Frog Mugs*

One of the most amusing jokes perpetrated by the potters was the frog mug, a drinking vessel of quite normal and innocent appearance which concealed a slimy frog which became visible only as the unsuspecting drinker drained his pot. As the earliest surviving frog mugs are all factory-made pieces of the 1775–80 period, it is probable that the coarse earthenware examples are descended from these, for none has been dated before the mid-nineteenth century. Even though frog mugs in plain and agate wares were made in Sussex, the major country potteries to produce them were undoubtedly those in Yorkshire, round Halifax. As G. Dent wrote in 1931,[21] 'At one time, some years back, nearly all the public houses about Halifax had one or more of these "Frog" mugs... Some of the frogs have an opening in the mouth so that, when a person is drinking, the liquor pours out from the aperture.' All the Halifax frog mugs housed in the various local museums are firmly provenanced products of the Howcans Pottery, the similarity of their styles and modelling adding conviction to the suggestion that this was the major, if not the only, pottery to make them in this area. They all have cylindrical redware bodies finished with a plain bead round the base, two looped handles and a distinctive frog made from a sloping cone of light-coloured clay with a wide knife-cut mouth, dark applied-clay eyes and feet finished off as round pads scored to represent the phalanges. One of the earliest, inscribed J+R+C.S. 1861', is in the Yorkshire Museum at York (no. 64/a), its only unusual features being the use of white sprig-moulded motifs showing the royal arms, a seated man with a dog by his side and a shell pattern round the exterior, and the substitution of an agate-ware fabric for the frog instead of the usual white. The later examples are much more uniform, however, as is seen in a piece in the Halifax Museums' collection inscribed 'I.L.1889'. The 1889 mug is particularly interesting, for across its base runs the contemporary pencil inscription 'Last kiln at Howcans, 1889'. This proves it to be one of the last batch of Halifax frog mugs to be made, and so suggests that all similar pieces should at least pre-date it.

*Notes for this chapter are on pages 178–9*

## *Chapter Seven*

# *Kitchen and Table*

However interesting we may find the puzzle jugs, harvest wares, or money boxes made by the country potter, it is well to remember that these wares were the rare elements in his production, the pieces made specifically for a particular person or occasion. The real mainstay of the country potter's existence lay in the provision of domestic wares for, in common with the coopers and turners, he played an important role in providing the housewife with the equipment necessary to preserve, prepare and serve her food. This preoccupation with the functional aspects of his craft did not mean that the potter's wares were either dull or offensively well-styled, as is often the case today. It is almost impossible to find a poor shape, a weak handle, or a major functional design fault in any piece of country pottery, for as he had close personal contact with his customers both at the pottery, on the pot-cart, or in the market place, he would soon have heard if his wares were unsatisfactory and he would have lost trade accordingly.

To appreciate the pieces made for domestic use it is advisable to gain some knowledge of the functions they served, as this adds considerably to their interest.

## *Brewing*

Perhaps the largest wares ever to be made in any quantity by the English coarseware potters were the huge brewing jars used in the northern counties from the early nineteenth century onwards. Traditionally beer was always brewed in large metal boilers which were permanently mounted in masonry sheaths containing a fireplace, a spiral flue, and a tall chimney. Such arrangements were suitable only for fairly large establishments, however, being too expensive to install or operate in smaller households. With the expansion of the urban populations a growing demand for small-scale brewing utensils developed. To meet this demand the potters began to make lead-glazed brewing jars of up to 72gal (ie, two barrels) capacity. In 1830 the Beer-house Act was passed, its effect being to make beer more readily available than before, and consequently to make the time-consuming operation of home-brewing much less attractive. By the third quarter of the nineteenth century over 95 per cent of Britain's beer was being produced commercially, and so the demand for brewing jars ceased entirely.

The technique of brewing consisted, briefly, of mashing malt in warm water, allowing it to stand, draining off the sweet wort, boiling the wort with hops and fermenting the resultant liquor with a yeast culture to form beer. The jars were used chiefly for the initial process of mashing, an example in the Tolson Memorial Museum at Huddersfield being used by Mrs Whitaker of Cliff Hill, Cawthorne, as her 'mash-tub'.

Although all brewing jars possessed a wide mouth and a spiggot-hole near the base, their individual designs varied from one area to another, thus making it possible to determine their origins with a fair degree of accuracy. In the north east, particularly in the Tyne Valley, they took the form of large convex-sided pots measuring up to 3ft in height and 2ft in diameter. Round their widest points two, four, or even six horizontal handles were applied to enable them to be lifted, while their sloping surfaces above the handles were decorated with parallel bands of white slip trailed over the red fabrics. The brewing jars of the West Riding of Yorkshire took two rather different forms, the first having a relatively straight-sided body with sides tapering from a particularly wide mouth

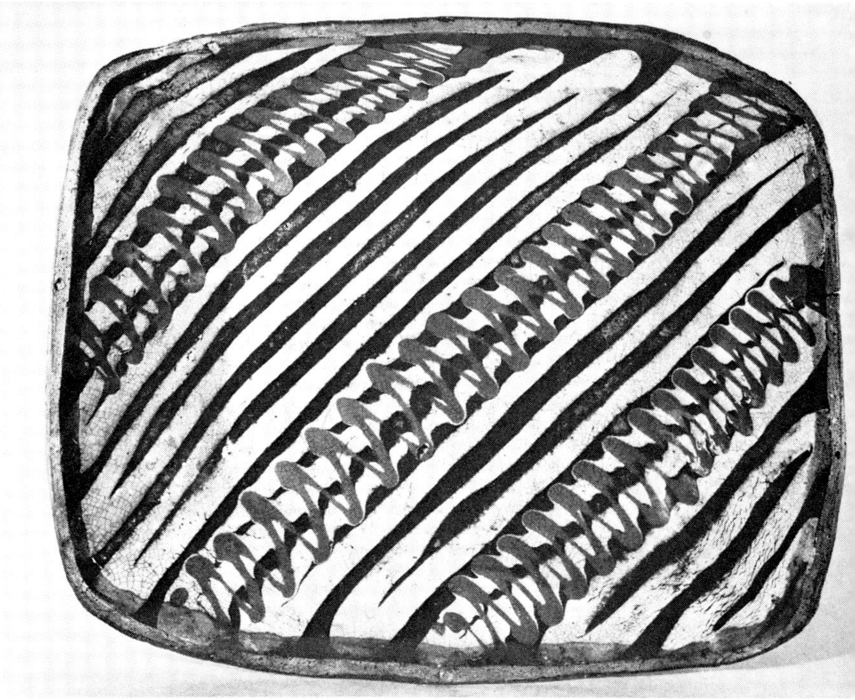

*Page 125* Pressed-ware dishes; the example from Polesworth Pottery (*above*) was decorated before being shaped, while the Tyneside dish (*below*) had its slip trailed when almost finished (see notes on page 184)

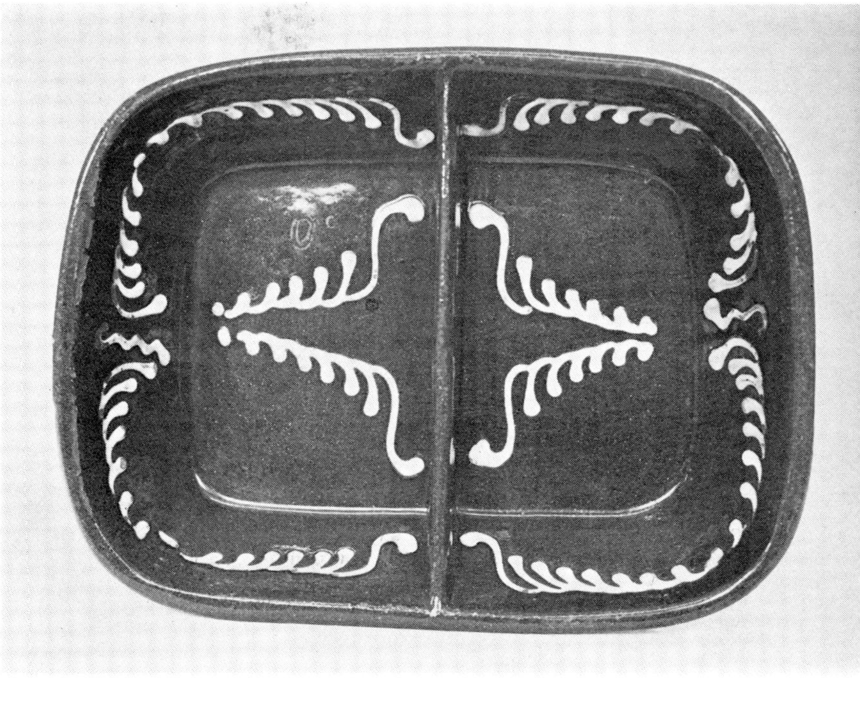

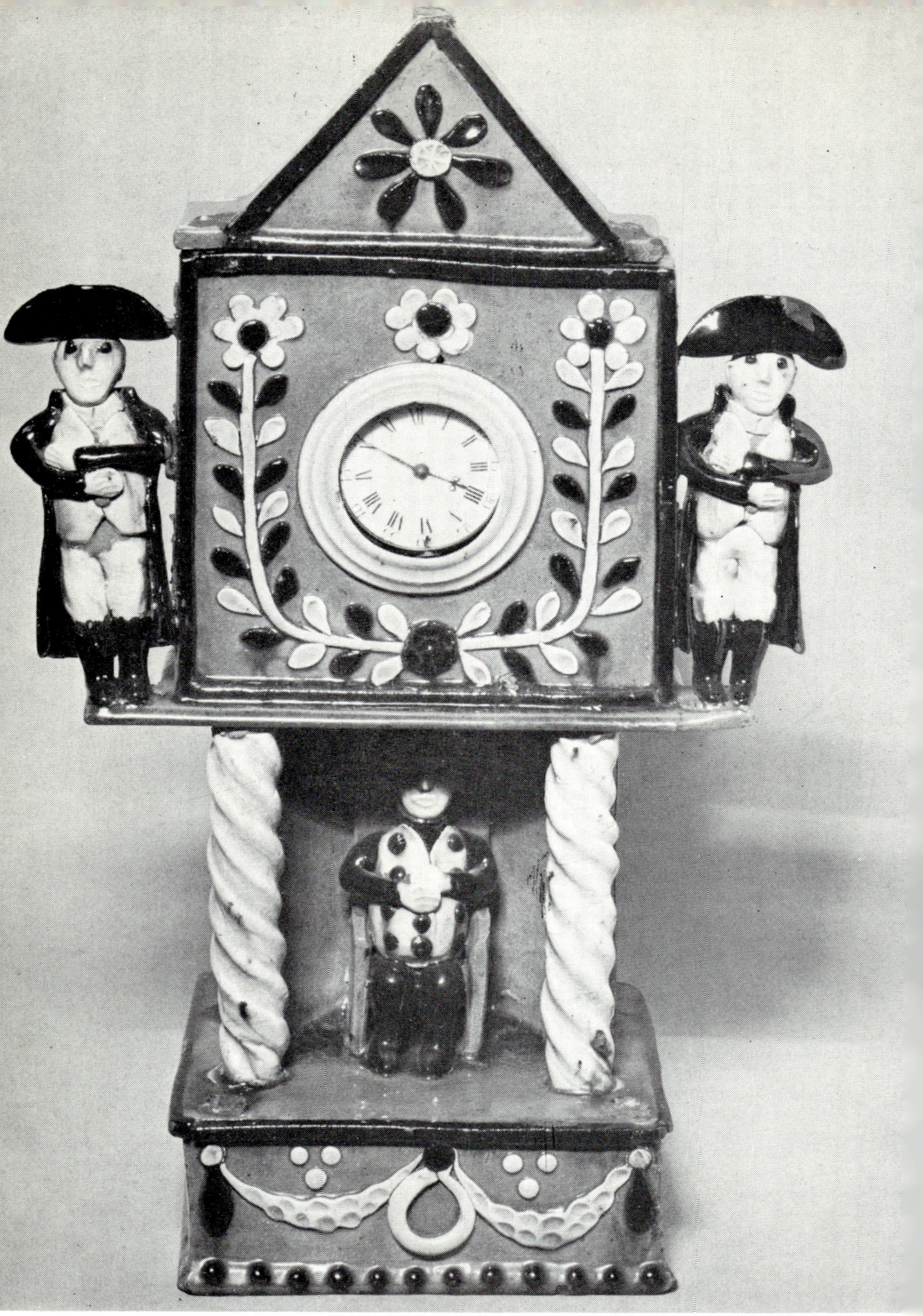

*Page 126* A magnificent watch-pocket made by George Fishley of Fremington (1771–1856) (see notes on page 184)

down to a slightly smaller base. A pot of this type was used by the Kent family in their brewhouse at Tatefield Hall near Harrogate, its red fabric being covered in an almost metallic black iron-stained glaze. Other examples from Keighley and Cawthorne are also known, the latter being glazed to a pale orange-brown colour. The second variety, made in Halifax potteries, reached an immense size, the upper and lower halves of their broad convex bodies frequently being thrown separately and later joined together when dry. Often the middle joint was so carefully disguised that it is very difficult to trace, but on others the potters finished the joint with a semi-ornamental band of indented thumb-prints. Excellent examples of both these types are to be seen in the Folk Museum of West Yorkshire at Shibden Hall, Halifax.

## *Cutlery Boxes*

These most useful wares appear to have been made in Yorkshire alone, as no provenanced examples have yet been identified from outside that county. The earliest surviving box is undoubtedly the one now preserved in the Yorkshire Museum, York (no. 72/a), which was made at the Baggalay Pottery, Burton-in-Lonsdale for 'Knives & Forks 1797', as the inscription neatly trailed across the pot's front face clearly states. These early boxes were slab-built to the design of their high-class wooden contemporaries; a tall flat back, narrow sides, and rounded front all topped by a steeply-sloping lid are their major characteristics. No doubt the dark brown fabric enriched with its white trailing suggested mahogany with an ivory inlay, and it was all the more desirable for this.

Nearly all the later boxes were made in the Howcans and Soil Hill Potteries at Halifax during the third quarter of last century. They too copied the designs of wooden originals, but this time they took their pattern from the shallow knife-tray of the everyday farm kitchen. The Soil Hill examples, probably slab-built by Samuel Catherall himself, have plain box-shaped bases measuring approximately 12in by 9in, by $3\frac{1}{2}$in in height. Passing longitudinally along this base runs a central division, its upper edge rising in a shallow arc to form a handle for the whole pot. At this pottery the decoration and workmanship are not always of the highest order, and the wares are often quite dull in their design and finish. This can certainly be said of a cutlery box now in the Yorkshire Museum (no. 71/b) and made at Soil Hill in 1872. Its orange-red fabric is poorly glazed, while the decoration, here consisting of white dots stamped with a circular motif, a single face-mask on one side and the initials 'J.M.S. 1872' on the other, is very poorly executed. A similar example is also to be seen in the Glaisher Collection at Cambridge (no. 399); it has a twisted loop handle and the date 'AGUST 24 1865'. The boxes made at the Howcans Pottery were of a vastly superior type and can easily be distinguished from those of Soil Hill. Their bodies are usually a little larger, measuring perhaps 14in long by 10in in width, but their major differences lie in the details of the handle, with its curving, horn-shaped terminals, in the quatrefoil and S-shaped piercing through the vertical walls, in the heavy square-sectioned rim and in the high-quality inlaid work which decorates every surface. A fine example in the Yorkshire Museum (no. 71/a) has simple tree-motifs in the centre of each side wall, zig-zags round the rim, and curving tendril patterns round the walls and handle, all inlaid in white clay into a richly glazed mid-brown fabric. This piece, dated 1858, is almost identical to another Howcans piece in Shibden Hall, Halifax, the only differences being in the inlaying of white clay into the S-shaped piercing, and in the year of manufacture, 1853.

## *The Dairy*

Coarse hand-thrown earthenware was ideal for dairy use, its hard glazes maintaining a smooth and easily cleaned surface. Because of the comparative uniformity of dairying techniques, the design of these vessels changed very little from one part of the country to another, so the collector can identify his pieces only from the appearance of their materials. Once the milk had entered the dairy, one of the first tasks was to remove its cream, perhaps for butter-making. This was invariably done by allowing the milk to settle in a large milk pan, a shallow dish approximately 18in in diameter by 6in in height, its straight sides tapering down from the rim to a fairly small base. Here the milk would stand overnight, the cream rising to form a thick surface layer which could then be skimmed off into a separate container.

If butter was to be made the cream would be accumulated in a lidded cream pot before churning. The cream pot was usually a short convex-sided vessel, ranging for 9in or 10in up to perhaps 2ft in its overall height. At its shoulder two horizontal handles were applied to enable it to be lifted, while its deep rim was often pulled out to form a wide pouring lip. When enough cream had been prepared, it would be poured into the churn, where it was agitated for some time before it separated into butter and the thin, watery buttermilk. Up to the early to mid-nineteenth century most churns were cooper-made from oak staves bound with iron, but from that time onwards many potters began to produce ceramic examples based on the existing wooden shapes. In every case the potters copied the designs of the traditional plunge-churn, the tapering body having two handles applied to its sides, and a thrown lid; its tubular knob was opened out like a cup at the top so as to catch any milk which might splash from the reciprocating dasher. Once the butter was made it was scooped from the churn and kneaded or beaten in a container of either sycamore or elm, the scalded surfaces resisting its adhering fats far better than those of glazed earthenware. If the butter was to be preserved or packed for sale, it then had to be beaten into tubs or butter-pots, coarse salt being sprinkled between each layer as it was knuckled down firmly to exclude all pockets of air. This technique of storage has been in common use for a considerable period; Dr Robert Plot informs us in his *Natural History of Staffordshire* of 1677 that: 'The Butter they buy by the *Pot* of a long cylindrical form, made at *Burslem* in this country of a certain size, so as not to weigh above six pounds at most, and yet to contain at least 14 pound of Butter according to an Act of Parliament made about 14 or 16 years agoe, for regulateingg the abuses of this trade in the making of Pots, and false packing of the Butter.'

These early butter pots were made in a coarse grey-buff fabric which was totally impervious to water, even though it was unglazed. This non-porous quality was of great importance, for without it an unscrupulous dealer could easily damp down a short-weight pot to make it weigh the correct amount at the time of sale. Seventeenth-century butter pots of this type are extremely rare, very few being known outside museum collections. Later examples are much more common, however, for although the Act regulating their capacity and weight was allowed to lapse into disuse, the practice of preserving butter in this manner continued in some farms up to the 1940s. The pots made from the early and mid-eighteenth century onwards were nearly all of a cylindrical form, although some tended to taper slightly towards the base; they usually measured between 12in to 18in in height by about 12in in diameter. They nearly all had two horizontal handles applied firmly beneath the rim, and they also had a rolled moulding extending round their upper edges, this being particularly useful when any form of protective covering had to be tied down.

Cheese-making, one of the most important dairy processes, required very little from the country potter, the vats and other equipment all being cooper-made to withstand the great pressure applied to them under the cheese-press. In the Halifax area, however, the potters did make a number of ceramic vats in which small, lightly pressed cheeses could be formed. These black-glazed pots are almost cylindrical, being approximately 9in in height by 7in in diameter at the rim, their bases being perhaps 1in narrower. With the exception of a plain area just below the rim, the body of each pot is pierced by rows of ¼in-diameter holes, three small feet raising the base so that the whey could drain easily from this area. When making a cheese the milk was first heated to blood heat and rennet or 'keslops' added to make it curdle. Once a hard curd had formed, it was broken and packed into a muslin cheese-cloth lining the vat and a heavy inch-thick lid placed on top of it to squeeze out the surplus whey so as to convert the loose curds into a moderately hard cheese.

## *Dishes*

Ever since the late seventeenth century the large flat faces of dishes and plates have attracted the decorative skills of the earthenware potter. Many early plates appear to have been specifically for display, for the wares of the Tofts and their numerous contemporaries are decorated to an incredibly high standard, motifs such as royal portraits, coats of arms, or biblical figures being used to demonstrate their owner's patriotic or religious leanings. Wares of this type have been studied in great detail elsewhere,[1] and so will not be dealt with here. Instead, this section will be concerned with those dishes which were made for everyday use in the home.

Most of the dishes made during the last two hundred years were pressed-wares, being formed from thin sheets of clay decorated with complicated slip designs, allowed to become half-dry, and then pressed into their final forms over mushroom-shaped moulds of either unglazed pottery or plaster of Paris. Frequently they were used as either meat or baking dishes, regularly being heated up to fairly high temperatures in the domestic oven. Joseph Kenworthy, for example, has recorded how George Hawksworth of Upper Midhope near Sheffield 'could remember his mother using a large and handsome slip-decorated dish for making Yorkshire puddings in . . . she used it with great reluctance, as if it had seen better days',[2] this probably took place about the middle of last century. From their inscriptions it can be seen that they were occasionally used for other purposes too, for one rectangular dish in the Sheffield City Museum has the word 'Money' trailed across its face; it probably served as an alms-dish or collecting tray at a local place of worship. Unfortunately there are very few well-provenanced dishes in existence today, and in consequence it is almost impossible to attribute a piece to a particular pottery with any degree of certainty. Some areas do have clear distinguishing features, however. In the Tyneside potteries the dishes were either oval or of rectangular plan with straight sides and rounded corners during the nineteenth century. A central division was also common here, in the form of a wall of clay running across the dish from the centre of one long side to the centre of the other. The coarse red fabric was always of a brick-red colour, sometimes slightly flecked with tiny white impurities, and showing as a mid-brown beneath the glossy glaze, which ceases about 2in down its outer surfaces. Frequently dishes of this type were decorated with white slip 'sprays' trailed in sloping comma-like dashes inside their rims and bases, a feature unique to the Tyne Valley. Some examples also bear impressed marks such as 'FIREPROOF' or, more helpfully, 'Stepney Pottery, Newcastle upon Tyne, Fire Proof' in a copper-plate typeface, this being the mark used by John Wood & Co of Stepney Bank, Ouseburn, from about 1877 to 1912. Due to the extensive coastal trade from Newcastle, these dishes are to be found in most of the eastern counties; the Yarmouth Museums, for example, have a magnificent specimen over 2ft in length which was shipped down into Norfolk soon after it was made. Other Tyneside dishes were shipped even greater distances, however, as was recently proved when archaeologists working at St Augustine, Florida, excavated an oval example bearing the usual white slip sprays and the date 1813 from one of their sites.

A little further south, at the Clarence Potteries, Norton, Stockton-on-Tees, Thomas Harwood and his successors produced a range of rectangular meat dishes for butchers between 1850 and 1895, the title of 'Welsh trays' being given to them here. Made in a near-white fabric, their upper surfaces were decorated with beautifully trailed and feathered designs in pale-blue, dark-brown, and white slips. Most of these plates are unmarked, but occasionally they bear the impressed sign 'HARWOOD'; this indicates an early date of manufacture, as Thomas Harwood's trustees sold the pottery to a limited company shortly after his death.

In north-west Yorkshire the potters of Burton-in-Lonsdale made shallow dishes or plates in their typical dark-red fabric, but these are extremely rare, only one provenanced example being known. This is no. 405 in the Glaisher Collection, an 8in-diameter plate purchased along with two other 'Black Burton' pieces from a woman in Barrow-in-Furness early in the twentieth century. As might be expected, its decoration is carefully trailed in white slip; a central rectangular panel bears the inscriptions 'W T & G' and '1793' placed respectively above and below a transverse line, while a row of curved 'petals' continues as a border round its rim. Plates from the Halifax potteries are similarly scarce, for, with the exception of the plain brown-glazed plates made by Nicholas Taylor of the Denholme Pottery as part of his tea sets, no well-provenanced examples have survived. Excavations on the precipitous site of the eighteenth-century pottery of the Halliday family at Bate Hayne, just north of Halifax, have shown that small round dishes were made there in a cream fabric coated on their upper surfaces with a dark red-brown iron slip, white slip-trailed decoration and a pale-yellow lead glaze.

The Midhope potteries, situated in the Little Don Valley to the north-west of Sheffield, made a great variety of large circular slipware plates from the eighteenth century to the early nineteenth, when the major slipware potter working there died. A large collection of sherds excavated from the Midhope sites is now in the Kenworthy Collection at the Weston Park Museum at Sheffield. Some of the designs are identical to those of the contemporary Staffordshire potteries, where they were undoubtedly made, but others are quite different in their methods of trailing and are presumably genuine Midhope products. Most of these have notched rims and their patterns are formed from fine slipware linework trailed and feathered in cream, light-brown and dark red-brown slips over a hard-fired pale-buff fabric. They may be classified as follows:

1 Parallel patterns, in which the surface of the dish is covered with numerous closely trailed lines of coloured slip. Often the design is broken up by wide bands of white slip along which run either broad zig-zag lines or else large dots, the latter being pulled out to a heart shape with a bristle while still wet. The parallel lines are usually feathered with bristle strokes running in alternate directions at 90 or 45 degrees to the pattern, thus producing a very delicate and interesting surface appearance.

2 Grid patterns, where dark-brown slips are first trailed across the cream-slipped dish in groups of three or four parallel lines; these are broken up by having single or double lines trailed across them at regular intervals in opposite directions, to give a regular grid-like pattern.

3 Marbled patterns, where slips of different colours are first trailed across the surface before being swirled together to give a rich marble-like finish.

4 Floral patterns, consisting of white outline designs of leaves, tulips or roses trailed in a fluid style over a dark-brown background, light-brown slip frequently being used to infill leaf centres or flower details and so on.

Very similar wares were made in Derbyshire in the potteries at Ticknall and at Bolsover, many pieces being attributed to these sites, though there are very few pots with proven Derbyshire origins. The only dish known to have come from Ticknall is now in the Greg Collection at Manchester (no. 41), its reputation resting solely on the strength of its old paper label, which states: 'Tickenhall "Slip Ware", Derbyshire—This ... was purchased about 25 years ago [*c.* 1869] by J. J. Briggs, the neighbourhood of Tickenhall, from an old servant of his [in] whose family it had been for many years, and had been known to him some years prior to him purchasing it....' Hardly an indisputable history, but considering its style and materials, and also the fact that it was certainly in the hands of a family from the Ticknall area, it may be assumed to be a Ticknall piece of eighteenth or possibly even early nineteenth-century date. The dish itself has a deep-buff fabric covered with a dark red-brown slip, and is decorated with three hounds chasing a fox by a tree; these features have white slip outlines with light-brown slip details, and these colours are repeated in five crescents of alternate plain and wavy lines which form a partial border to the notched rim. Materials of the same type were also employed at the Bolsover Pottery, which closed in 1749. During the early 1890s, when an area near the market place in Bolsover was being cleared for redevelopment, the site of the old pottery was discovered, and sherds of the wares formerly made there were collected and deposited in the British Museum (no. D 48) and in Nottingham and Derby Museums. These indicate that the buff-fabric wares made here were coated with dark-brown, white and light-brown slips.

In Staffordshire the attribution of plates and dishes to particular potters or potteries is equally difficult for not all late seventeenth- and early eighteenth-century pieces bear the names or initials of their makers. It is usually possible to identify a Staffordshire product by the high quality of its manufacture, while such features as jewelled slip-trailing, cross-hatched slip borders or raised designs and inscriptions formed from grooves cut into the mushroom-shaped press-moulds almost guarantee a Staffordshire origin. As these wares have recently formed the major subject of R. G. Cooper's beautifully illustrated *English Slipware Dishes 1650–1850,* they are not discussed here.

The only other site at present believed to have made pressed-ware dishes in England was that at Polesworth in Warwickshire. The sole evidence currently available for a pottery here is provided by a jug in the Glaisher Collection (no. 365) which has the inscription 'POLESWORTH POTTERY 1800' trailed in dark-red slip round its buff body. A short time ago a plate made of identical materials was ploughed up at Polesworth, presumably being a product of the pottery there. It is rectangular in shape, with rounded corners and a design of white stripes trailed diagonally over the dark-red slip which covers the entire upper surface of its buff fabric. This is made a little more interesting by the addition of three tightly zig-zagging lines of light-red slip (perhaps a mixture of the dark-red and the white) which run parallel to the original design (see page 125).

Throughout southern England the techniques of making pressed flatwares were almost entirely unknown, the dishes and plates being either thrown or formed from basic thrown shapes. By northern standards the decoration was usually rather limited, too, the vast majority of the flatwares being completely plain. During the seventeenth century plates of a comparatively high quality had been made at a number of important pottery centres, but as the eighteenth century progressed their standards dropped. At Wrotham plates went out of production entirely; at Donyatt the excellent sgraffito wares bearing human figures, cockerels or sun and tulip motifs (as seen in the County Museum at Taunton, Somerset) degenerated to a fairly low order, while at Barnstaple and Bideford in north Devon only one potter continued to make plates of an acceptable decorative standard in the 1740s.[3] His sgraffito wares have much in common with the better-known harvest jugs of the area, incorporating such designs as figures standing beneath a large symmetrical tree holding two birds, or else the royal arms, complete with their mottoes and supporters. The broad rims of these plates are always filled with a continuous border of white triangles (identical to those seen round the necks of most north Devon jugs), the darker areas between them being decorated with single quatrefoils. Stylistic comparisons with the harvest jugs of known north Devon potters show that these plates were undoubtedly the work of John Philips of Bideford, the identical royal arms appearing on his magnificent jug in the Athenaeum at Barnstaple. In the late nineteenth century another north Devon man, Edwin Beer Fishley of Fremington, again made plates of high quality, but instead of using sgraffito methods, scratching away the dry slip, he used the earlier combing technique, which involved a whalebone comb tipped with the teats from babies' dummies opening a series of soft wavy lines through the liquid coating of white slip. One of these plates in the Royal Albert Memorial Museum at Exeter (no. 76/1928/7) has the typical north Devon fabric covered with a white slip and a grass-green glaze. The quality of its execution is good, but its great beauty lies in the freedom and simplicity of its design.

## *Lighting*

One of the earliest forms of lamp consisted of a shallow oil-filled bowl from which a submerged wick projected slightly; this would give quite a reasonable light if carefully tended. Stone lamps of this type some fifteen thousand years old have been found in the caves of Lascaux in France but, rather surprisingly, pottery lamps working on this principle were still being used in England up to the end of the nineteenth century. These were the chills of Cornwall (see fig 13), which were thrown in the form of a shallow bowl with a narrow pinched-out spout. This was attached to the top of a tall shaft round which extended a wide base which gave the lamp stability, besides acting as a drip-tray for the surplus oil from the lamp above. In use, the bowl was filled with the train oil which was extracted from pilchards by the local fishwives, who brought it to the markets in large earthenware jars. A 'purvan' or wick of either rush or cotton, or else a 'booba' of plaited linen strips, was then dipped into the oil, one end extending above the surface within the narrow spout.

In the remainder of the country the potter was frequently called upon to produce candlesticks, the low price, attractive finish and fireproof qualities of earthenware making it particularly suitable for this purpose. Most of these candlesticks were quite undistinguished, but a few were of outstanding quality and can easily be identified. With the exception of Edwin Beer Fishley's skilful reproductions of Wrotham pieces, which are easily detected by the conspicuous colour of their clay, the most interesting examples were undoubtedly those

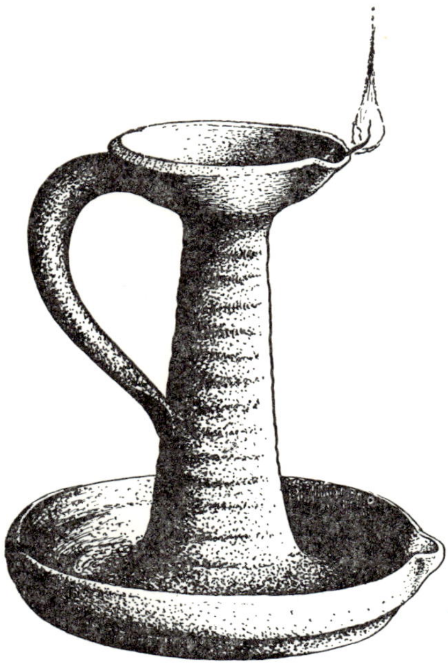

Fig 13 A Cornish chill made in the early nineteenth century

made at the Ginns Pottery at Whitehaven by John Kitchin. Dating from the 1850s, they are extremely bold and startling in their design. One stick formerly in the possession of the Kitchin family takes the form of a cylindrical agate-ware lantern, its sides being pierced by a large square aperture above which flock numerous small birds, apparently attracted by the light. Above this, round the top of the lantern, are spaced white candle holders, their tops being cut in small scallops to give a particularly rich effect. Most surprising of all is a tall spire thrown with skilfully cut white and agate-ware flanges which rises above the lantern to support a single hen finial on top. It is an extremely interesting piece, totally unlike anything produced elsewhere, both in its concept and in its techniques. It is possible that the same pottery was responsible for an unprovenanced candlestick-inkwell in the collection of Stoke-on-Trent City Museum (no. 602 P 44). This has a low agate-ware base, round in plan, with three pen-holes cut through its upper surface into the torroidal ink chamber which encircles a slightly taller pen-holder in the centre. To one side rises a candlestick in white clay, its interesting silhouette giving it the appearance of an early locomotive chimney. Besides the similarity of the materials, the neat scalloping of the thrown surfaces and the novel combination of the two functions suggest that this may be a Whitehaven piece.

Besides making candlesticks the Soil Hill Pottery near Halifax also made a range of wall-mounted candle holders which were available in a variety of patterns. All these were probably made by Samuel Catherall (1807–87), for the slip-trailed motifs which appear on the candle holders also occur on some of his signed pieces, including his signed plant pots now in the Yorkshire Museum at York (e.g. no. 88/a). They always consist of a vertical circle of thrown clay some 11in in diameter, on the front of which is mounted a 4in-diameter cylindrical pot, this latter section being used to hold the candles. One redware example in the Yorkshire Museum (no. 75/a) has been deeply notched round the edge of its back panel so as to resemble a large gear-wheel; it is decorated with zig-zag and circle designs in trailed slip, while on the front appears a white sprig-moulded face above the initials 'T.E.H. 1871'. Examples are known in private collections which have a border of ½in-diameter balls of white clay applied round their perimeter and simple slip-trailed dates ranging through the 1860s and 1870s.

## *Mugs*

By the early eighteenth century the mug had become quite an important item of domestic ware, having passed through numerous stages of development since its introduction over two hundred years earlier. It was used to hold almost any kind of liquid food or drink, frequently taking the place of the bowl for soups, stews or porridge, and was to be found in most households. Owing to the normal everyday usage to which these wares were subject, their life expectancy was extremely short and, with few exceptions, it is only the finer inscribed pieces which have survived up to the present day.

In Yorkshire a number of plain pint or 1½pt mugs with red or buff fabrics and glossy black iron-stained glazes have survived in both public and private hands. These are the mease or meeas pots, round-bodied vessels opening a little at the mouth and with a single looped handle just large enough to receive the crooked index finger. Although they were often used up to the 1900s in some houses, their most popular period of use was the eighteenth and early nineteenth centuries. In the south-western corner of the county the locally made Midhope mease pots were always used after the annual service of the Bolsterstone Club (a friendly society) when the members adjourned to the Castle Inn where

> It was, of course, impossible to seat and serve them all at one sitting, so, to mitigate the inconvenience of hunger waiting too long on expectation, the landlord placed a manservant at a large table in the lower room, whose duty it was to break up several stones of oat-cake into suitable pieces and put them into broth. The table was covered, on these occasions, with meeas-pots, all steaming with a good measure of delicious broth, which was served out to those from afar as a 'biting on' whilst waiting their turn for the dinner propper. On the evolution of better arrangements, this custom fell into desuetude, and the broth, with its complement of oat-cake, was distributed to poor neighbours who thronged around the kitchen door at the close of the feast with the request 'Pray, dame! will yo gie me a meeas o' broth?'[4]

In other parts of the country similar vessels were made in their own local styles, their fabrics alone giving any clues as to their origins. The close grain, pale colour and fine throwing of a cylindrical mug may suggest a Sussex source, for example (see the Stoke-on-Trent City Museum no. 53 P 51), just as a shallow mug with a light orange-brown fabric, white slip and yellow glaze with green patches, inscribed 'Remember thow keep holy the Sabath Day R A 1722' in sgraffito is certainly from Donyatt (see an example in the County Museum at Taunton, Somerset).

A few mugs are so distinctive, as to enable their makers to be identified with little trouble. Such are the products of C. H. Brannam of Barnstaple, who in the late nineteenth century made a series of cylindrical two-handled mugs measuring about 5in in height by 4in in diameter. He always covered these redware pots with a coating of white slip, cutting inscriptions with pseudo-antique dates in sgraffito across their faces. Typical examples in the North Devon Athenaeum at Barnstaple and the Burton Art Gallery, Bideford (no. 333) bear such lines as:

Words are easy
Like the wind
Faithful friends
Are hard to find
1766

or

If ye can't lie aisy
Be as aisy
as ye
can
1821

Other distinctive mugs were made at Fremington by Edwin Beer Fishley and his grandson Fishley Holland, their wares being characterised by the usual north Devon fabric dipped into slip to produce a 1in-wide band round their rims, and the inscriptions: 'THE GIFT IS SMALL GOOD WILL IS ALL' or 'Fill me full of liquor sweet, for that is good when friends do meet/ when friends do meet and liquor plenty, Fill me again when I B M T', (see Royal Albert Memorial Museum, Exeter, nos. 67/1928/7 and 50/1960). Occasionally small white slip motifs were trailed over the bodies of the mugs, but perhaps their handles provided their other most noticeable feature. These were pulled by hand to a very high standard, great care being taken to finish off their joints, a circular thumb-piece often being added at the top, while the bottom usually rolled back on itself in a fine shelf-like scroll.

## *Posset Pots*

Posset was a drink made from hot milk curdled with ale, wine or lemon, a spicy flavour being imparted by the addition of sugar with cinnamon, ginger or nutmeg. From the medieval period onwards it formed an excellent nightcap for the family or friends; Pepys, for example, writes: 'After supper to dancing and singing till about twelve at night; and then we had a good sack-posset for them and an excellent cake.'[4] The posset pot was usually a two-handled vessel holding up to 7pt or 8pt of the beverage, the whole pot being passed from one drinker to another round the assembled company, thus dispensing with the necessity for cups. Many seventeenth-century examples are known from the potteries of Staffordshire and Wrotham, but provenanced pieces dating from the following two centuries are comparatively rare.

Of these older potting centres only Staffordshire continued to make a range of posset pots, most of them being beautifully decorated in the sgraffito technique. A fine example in the Glaisher Collection (no. 320) has its broad bell-shaped body regularly divided up into four horizontal rows of small rectangular compartments of white slip, the surface of each one being further decorated with either flowers or trellis designs in pale slate-blue brushwork. The initials 'I S' and the date '1764' are boldly cut into the front and rear panels of this pot, but even if this had not been done, the perfectly straight lines of the sgraffito and the overall high quality of the workmanship would have confirmed that this was a late eighteenth-century Staffordshire piece. A confident attribution is not always possible, however, for excavations have

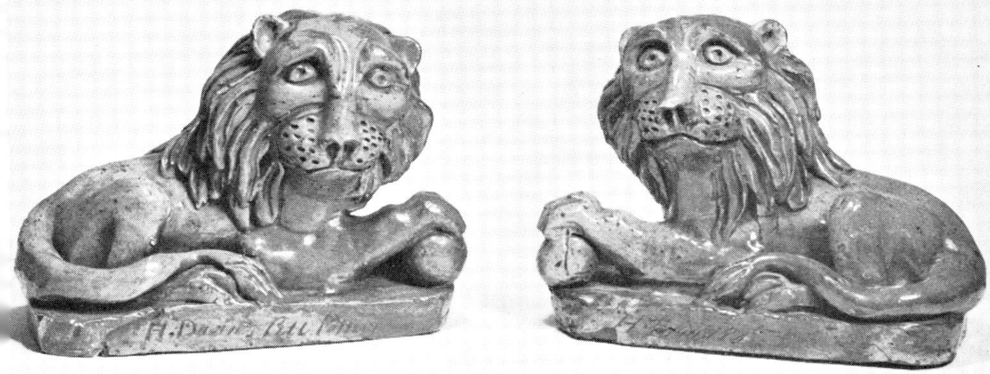

*Page 143* Models: the two lions (*above*) were made at the early to mid-nineteenth-century Pill Pottery, near Bristol, by H. Davies. He probably made the small cottage (*below*) at about the same time (see notes on pages 184–5)

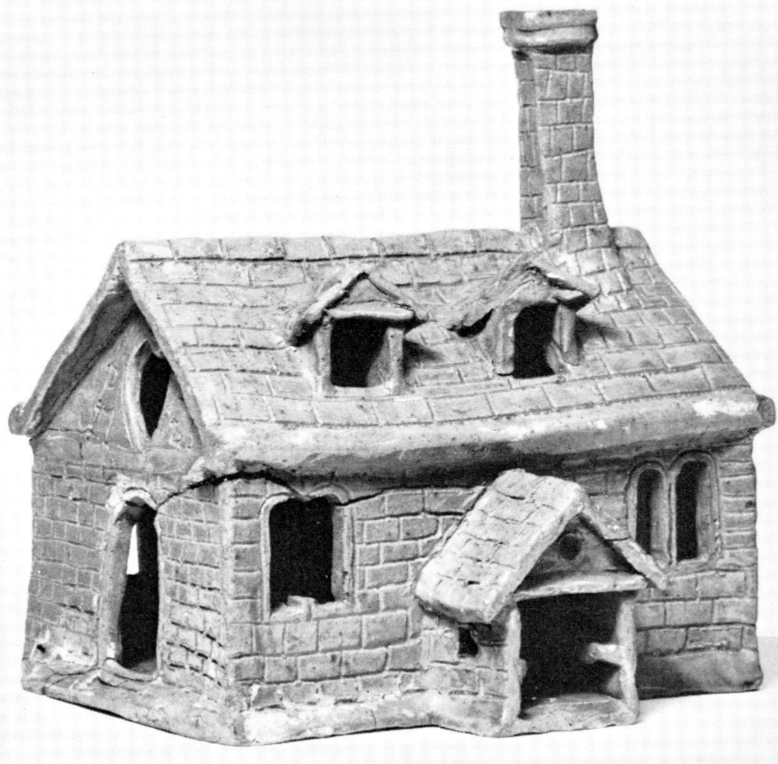

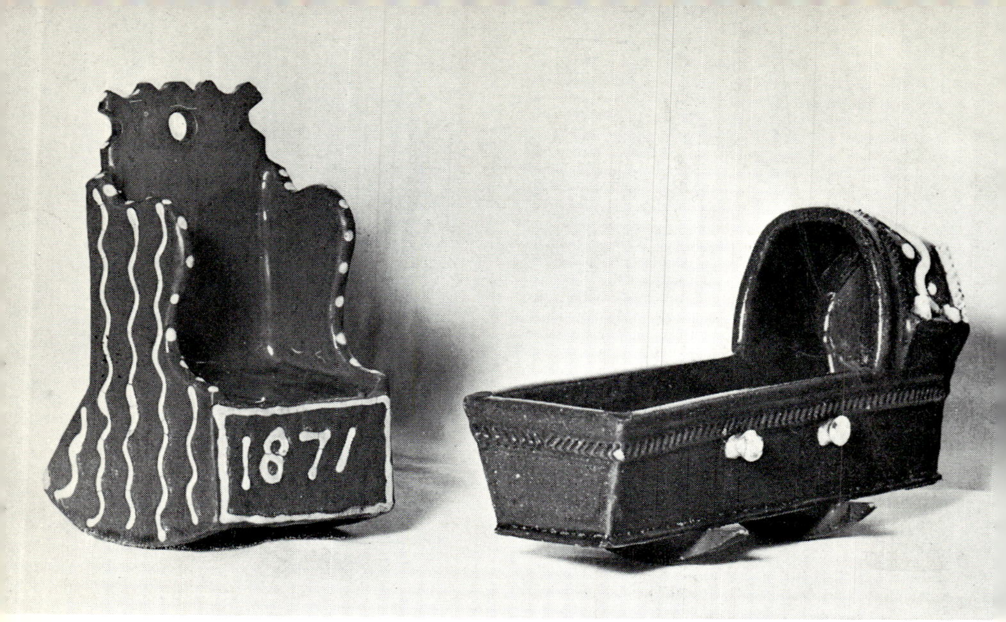


*Page 144* Model furniture: although the rocking chair (*above*) could have been made at a number of Halifax potteries, the cradle and chest of drawers both show the V-notched edges of the Woodman House Pottery (see notes on page 185)

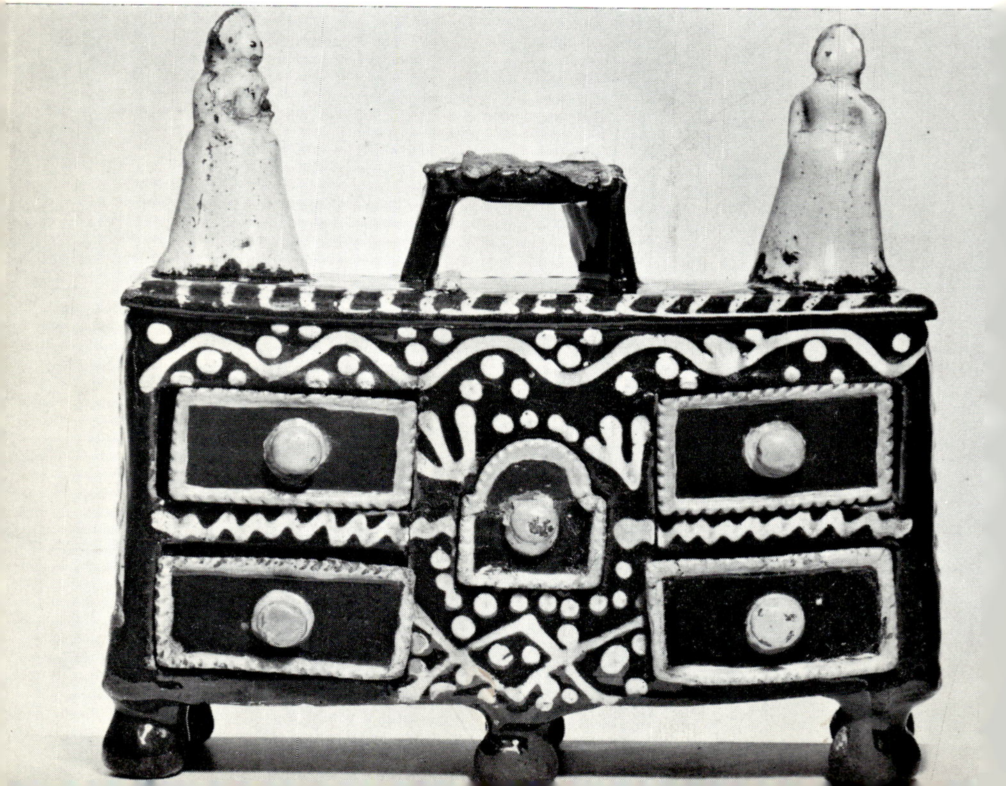

shown that many other so-called Staffordshire wares could easily have been made in Derbyshire or even in south Yorkshire. Typical of these are the other Glaisher posset pots (nos. 318 and 319). These both have a buff fabric coated in a dark-red slip and a yellow lead glaze, with crude tulip motifs and the inscriptions 'T B 1730' and 'W W 1732' showing through in a white-lined sgraffito. Both have a narrow tube modelled up the centre of their front faces between the handles, thus enabling the moustached drinker to suck up his posset without clogging his whiskers with the sweet spice-laden froth which topped the mixture. Similar materials are also to be seen in an immense four-handled posset pot (Glaisher no. 51) acquired at 'Barton-on-Trent quite near the Ticknall pottery' about the turn of the century, but instead of sgraffito, this one is decorated in white slip-trailing and is inscribed round its rim 'A Present for Thomas Bryan's Wife April 16th 1817'. It would be impossible to drink directly from such a huge vessel, so it was presumably used in the manner of a punch-bowl, the steaming contents being ladled out into smaller vessels for each individual guest.

The same materials were also used in the early to mid-eighteenth-century Halifax potteries, as is proved by the recent excavations on the site of the former Bate Hayne kilns of the Halliday family. The Folk Museum of West Yorkshire at Shibden Hall, Halifax houses a posset pot which probably originated here, its buff fabric, dark-red slip and lead glaze all being identical to the excavated sherds. In form it follows a thistle-shaped outline, its almost spherical lower half being topped by a wide flaring mouth. Instead of being decorated in a truly ceramic manner, this piece still bears its contemporary oil colour, gay cream and red brushwork depicting a lion and a unicorn over a crown at one side, while a variety of birds and flowers adorn the other. Just above one handle the owner's initials 'C. IA' and the date '1737' are added in red (see page 18), showing this to be the earliest Halifax posset pot extant. All the later posset pots from this area follow the same thistle-shaped pattern, but most of them rely on slip-trailing for decoration. Posset pots continued to be made in the Halifax potteries up to the 1820s at least, but the mid-nineteenth century saw a decline as possets became unfashionable. One of the latest examples to be made here is also in the Shibden Hall collection, this being of the usual Halifax thistle shape enriched with a wavy line and dotted daisy-pattern frieze above which is trailed 'G J + E 1825'.

The remainder of the identifiable posset pots from England all come from the southern counties, the major potteries each being represented by only one or perhaps two vessels. It is possible that there may still be good specimens in private hands, but for the moment our knowledge is limited to the examples described below. From north Devon comes a single bulbous pot with two loop handles and a wide flaring rim. Made in the usual light red-brown fabric of this area, its decoration is cut in sgraffito through an overall coating of white slip. On one side a thrush sits on a small branch, while on the other are inscribed the owner's name and the date 'John Hoolme, July 4th 1805' (Glaisher no. 63). Donyatt, too, is represented by a single example in the Somerset County Museum at Taunton, its style conclusively proving its origins. Round its body are spaced four loop handles, each separated from its neighbour by a small vertical ribbon of corrugated clay, while beneath its rim runs the line 'The gift is Small butt Love is all 1766' clearly cut through the white slip. The only posset pots from Sussex, meanwhile, are thrown to a bulbous form in a red iron-flecked Wealden clay, as is seen in the Glaisher Collection's no. 347. This has the initials 'F A B 1820' trailed in white amid frond and spray motifs to one side of its two handles, while at the other it states:

(whe)n this you see remember me
and keep me in your mind
leet all men still say what they will
speak of me ass you find
they rose is read they gras is green
this is my pot till I am dead.

## *Roasters*

Before the general introduction of the cast-iron cooking range from the mid- to late-eighteenth century onwards all cooking operations had to be carried out round the hearth, where the fire burnt either on andirons or in a basket grate. Most cooking vessels were made of either iron or brass, as these materials were able to withstand the direct heat of the flame, but in the embers or at a short distance from the fire, where the heat was less intense, pottery vessels were just as suitable. Perhaps the most interesting group of these vessels was the various types of Dutch oven or roaster in which meat or fruit could be placed close to the fire so as to cook in its radiant heat.

The earliest form of this vessel was made by members of the Wedgwood family of Yearsley in north Yorkshire. One of their products in the Yorkshire Museum at York (no. 57/a) was excavated from the site of the pottery in the middle of the nineteenth century. It consists of a 16in-diameter pot which has been sliced vertically in two to form a semi-circular vessel with an internal shelf and two external strap handles (see figure 14). It is made in a northern reduced greenware fabric which shows an olive green under a thick lead glaze and bears the incised inscription '1712 ATIC' across the upper half of its inner surface. A second example, now in the Castle Museum at York, is decorated with two incised birds, between which is cut the date '1726'. Potters operating a kiln within the ruins of Sheffield Manor in south Yorkshire also made roasters at this time, a particularly fine example being excavated recently from the pottery site. Now in the Weston Park Museum, Sheffield, it has a pale-buff fabric and a heavily speckled brown iron-stained glaze identical to that usually associated with Staffordshire. Its chief interest lies in the character of its decoration, for instead of having its curved back panel completely solid, it is pierced by six large triangular holes, the spandrels between these and the roaster's base each being ornamented with an incised cross surrounded by borders of 8in-diameter holes and straight incised lines. Of even greater interest, however, is the decoration incised into the glazed underside of its base. This consists of a wide freely cut tulip motif above which are placed the date '1715',

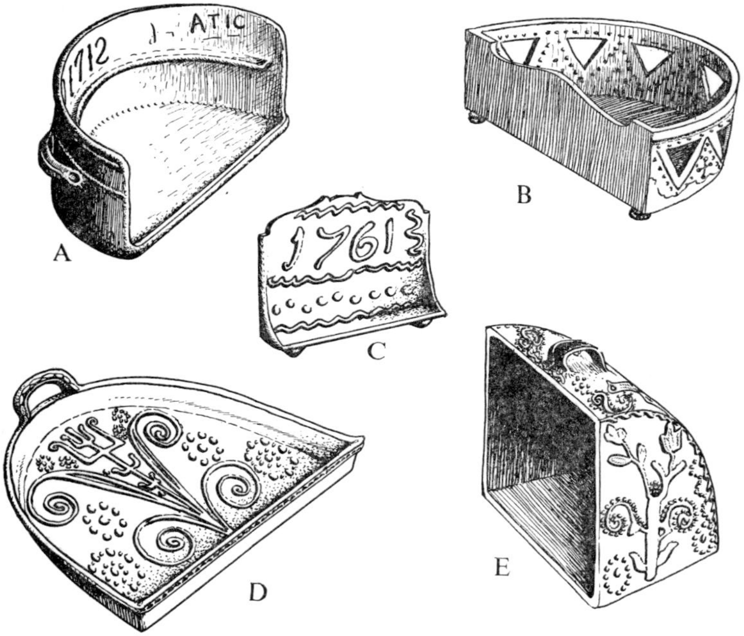


Fig 14 Roasters made in (A) Yearsley, Yorkshire, in 1712, (B) Sheffield, Yorkshire, in 1715, (C) Watchet, Somerset, in 1761 and (D and E) eighteenth-century Staffordshire

and the initials 'I.E.F.', the latter presumably standing for John Fox (and his wife E...?), son of Mary Fox (formerly Blackburn), owner of the pottery.

A number of similar undecorated vessels known as apple roasters were also used in Norfolk; the examples from Norwich and Great Yarmouth now in the Castle Museum at Norwich (nos. GYHE L.1965.1,331.967 and 163.949) have a pair of vertical loop handles attached to their curved back walls. They were also known in Somerset, but were modified here by the addition of a few shallow cups applied along the upper edges of their rims, these being used to hold individual apples before the fire.

In Staffordshire the roasters took on slightly different proportions, retaining the semi-circular plan, but with low walls of equal height passing round their entire perimeters. A fine example of this type is to be seen in the City Museum at Leicester (no. OS 70.1953). This has a single horizontal loop handle modelled on top of its curving rim, and its flat inner surface is enriched with a tulip pattern trailed in white slip over the coarse redware fabric. Other eighteenth-century ovens from Staffordshire were completely slab-built with a flat rectangular base some 10in long by 6in broad, quadrant-shaped vertical ends rising above this to support a curving back panel (see figure 14). These vessels are always made in a dark-red fabric decorated with white slip-trailed designs and the colours showed up a rich dark-brown and golden-yellow beneath the lead glaze. One example in the City Museum, Stoke-on-Trent bears a design composed of tulips in pots (no. 145P34), while another in the same collection (no. 412P50) is decorated with a symmetrical pair of perching pigeons. On closer examination the latter piece is found to have minute inscriptions scratched into its glaze at various points. Inside the front edge a copper-plate hand has written *'This Slipware Oven was made in Staffordshire A.D. 1741'*, but this is not to be taken at its face value, for underneath it states *'W. J. Naylor Liverpool July 1891 made at Cockpit Pottery Staffordshire 1741'*, and in front of the handle *'M. Haworth Liverpool 1791'*. Suspicion is at once aroused by the fact that all the inscriptions were written by the same person, in addition to which all the dates fall exactly into fifty-year units. Further research has shown that this oven was purchased from W. J. Naylor of Oswestry in 1950; it would therefore appear that Mr Naylor decided to record a fabricated history on the piece, giving it a pedigree which would have been quite convincing in 1891, though little weight should be placed on it today.

The Sussex roasters, of which only very few survive, were made in a completely different manner. Instead of being made either from slabs of clay or from cylindrical thrown shapes, they were formed from bottle-like pots strongly resembling the harvest bottles of that county with their almost spherical bodies. One of these, in the Victoria and Albert Museum (no. C21.1936), has the rich iron-speckled red-brown fabric usually associated with the Weald, and stands about 9in in height. Almost all the front half of the roaster has been sliced away to present a deep niched opening for the food, just enough fabric being left round the top to support a central knob, while a small handle is applied down the shoulder at the back.

Besides producing these larger vessels with their curved enclosing walls, two potteries also made small 'bacon roasters' with a simple flat back rising above a shallow rectangular drip tray. One of the earliest of these is in the British Museum (no. D 71), where it presents a good example of the plainer Staffordshire slip decoration, its red fabric being ornamented with a white slip tulip motif across its back, while the date 1692 is trailed along the bottom of the drip tray beneath. Very similar wares were being made in Somerset almost a century later, as is illustrated by two orange-brown examples in the Somerset County Museum in Taunton. One dated 1761 in cream slip has no certain provenance, but the other, dated 1783, has a well-documented history. According to information recorded in the museum's files, this roaster belonged to Mrs Welshire of The Croft, Crowcombe. She inherited it from her grandmother, who said it had been made at Watchet. Later, probably in the early twentieth century, Mrs Welshire gave it to Mrs Carew of Crowcombe Court, from whom it was acquired by Mrs Trollope-Bellow, who placed it in the museum in 1947. It is unusual to find such a complete history for a piece of country pottery, but as this is perhaps the only reference to a pottery at Watchet, it demonstrates the importance of recording all the available information regarding a piece as soon as it is acquired.

## *Salting*

During the eighteenth century when the urban potteries were becoming active the production of preserved foods was still an exclusively domestic process. Pork, ham and beef were still being salted down in most farmhouses, while fish was either smoked or salted in the coastal towns before being transported inland. For centuries the market for salting vessels had been in the hands of the coopers, who made numerous types of steeping vats in iron-bound oak; but as the urban potteries developed they evolved suitable techniques for making these large wares, eventually cornering this market for themselves.

For meat salting a variety of vessels were used, their individual names and shapes changing almost from one pottery to the next throughout the country. Most of them took the form of a vertical-sided glazed pan, either round or oval in plan and measuring up to 30in in length and up to 12in in height. In the north of England, particularly in Yorkshire, they were often made to a pear-shaped pattern to receive the whole hams for which the county was famous. The most usual method of salting began with the making of a brine by adding sufficient salt to the water to enable an egg or a potato to float in it. The joints of meat were then placed in the salting pan and allowed to soak in the brine for a month or more, after which they were wiped dry and hung, or possibly smoked, ready for use.

In Devon and Cornwall, in particular, salted pilchards formed one of the major articles of the diet, the local tin and copper miners often preferring them to fresh fish. Throughout the eighteenth century large numbers had been salted down by each family and, as the Rev R. Warner commented in his *Tour Through Cornwall* of 1809,

> Each cottager on average is wont to lay in about a thousand fish for winter use. The quantity of salt necessary is about seven pounds to a hundred fish. Till the late rise in the duty of that article salt might be procured at 1½d per lb. and the whole stock

cured at an expense of 8s. 9d. But *tempora mutantor*; salt is now increased to 4d. per lb., and a thousand fish cannot be cured under £1″3″4d., a sum of unattainable magnitude to a poor man who gets only 6s. or, at most 7s. per week for his labour.

The duty on salt was repealed in 1825, and salting was carried on in the south-west up to a few decades ago. The vessel used to salt pilchards was the bussa, a deep round pan with vertical sides and an internal glaze. These were made in most of the coastal potting centres such as Barnstaple, Bideford or Truro, often being shipped along the coast to the various harbours in which they were used. Whenever there was a glut of fish the demand for a fresh supply of bussas was intense, and local potters used to race each other down the coast with waggon-loads of new pots. Such races from Truro to Penzance or Newlyn were apparently always won by the Lake's pot-cart, for their competitor's horse insisted on halting outside each inn along the road, a habit it had acquired over some years of practice! To salt the pilchards a layer of salt was first spread in the bottom of the bussa; then came a layer of pilchards, followed by more salt and so on until the whole pot was full. A piece of flannel was then laid over the top to prevent them from going 'rusty', and a heavy stone placed on top of this to press the contents firmly down.

Salt was also used for many other household purposes of course, a pot of it always being kept ready for use in the kitchen. Here it could easily be spoiled by the moisture from the steaming pots or the smuts from a smoking chimney, and so, from the mid-eighteenth century, the potters of the northern counties began to make specially shaped vessels to keep it clean and dry. Before this most households had used 'kits' to hold their salt, these being small circular cooper-made tubs, but as these went out of use the title of salt kit was transferred to their earthenware successors. In form the pottery salt kit resembled a convex-sided bottle, the neck invariably being sealed off to form a knob on the top. Access to the salt was gained through a wide circular hand-hole pierced through the vessel's shoulder, this being furnished with a deeply hooded rim formed from a separately thrown section.

The earliest surviving salt kits were made in the Nottingham area by William Woodward, a piece bearing the inscription 'M W 1799' being presented by his descendants to the Castle Museum, Nottingham, while another almost identical example marked 'W W 1749' can now be seen in the Glaisher Collection at Cambridge (no. 153). These both have short redware bodies which are fairly square about the shoulders, with horizontal strap handles thumbed across their back surfaces. Their most interesting feature lies in their decoration, for instead of the usual slip-trailing these Nottingham salt kits are inlaid with fine white line-work. The top of the knob bears a neat daisy motif in this technique, while the body itself shows a large round rose sprouting from a bush of hatched foliage placed just below the central hand-hole at the front.

In Yorkshire the salt kit was probably adopted at a slightly later date, for none of those available for study today was made before the opening years of the nineteenth century. It is likely that a number of potteries in south Yorkshire and Derbyshire produced them for a period, but the only provenanced examples to have survived intact were all made in the Halifax area. Here, at the Hallidays' Howcans Pottery, they were made in the normal red-firing Halifax fabric, with wide circular mouths and plain thrown knobs, each vessel measuring about 9in in overall height (see Yorkshire Museum nos. 84/b and c). The oldest of these has the date 1802 trailed within a simple border beneath the hand-hole, while to each side there extends a series of alternate straight and wavy vertical stripes in white slip. The later example is similarly undistinguished in its decoration, having the inscription 'T M R 1857' trailed within a border of dots and arcs, the only other embellishment being a circle of slip crosses which passes around the hand-hole, each cross having a single white dot placed in the spaces between its extended arms. The Kitsons of the Ainley Top and Woodman House potteries to the south of Halifax also made redware salt kits, but instead of maintaining the tall bulging bodies and hooded hand-holes found elsewhere, they preferred to follow the lines of the locally made salt-glazed stoneware bottles (see p 107). Their sides were perfectly straight, with hard angular shoulders and tall concave necks, the hand-holes being formed by cutting a square hole through the upper section of each pot. This harshness was considerably softened by the addition of the Kitsons' unique form of decoration. Wide strips of white clay rouletted or cut with regular V-shaped notches pass round the hand-hole, continuing below to form a rectangular cartouche containing the inscription 'D + E 1847', while further strips are arranged in the pattern of potted plants to each side. Decoration of a much richer nature is reserved for the top of the kit, for here the potter, possibly Edward Kitson himself, has added a large white hen for a knob, her brood of ten brown or white chickens perching round her, each one being picked out with eyes, combs and wings of a contrasting clay. Most surprising of all, however, is a large curly-tailed brown dog which advances across the upper surface of the kit to challenge the hen sitting complacently at the top. Work of this quality is particularly rare, the exuberance evident in its modelling and composition confirming that this pottery was surely responsible for some of the most exciting pieces of English country pottery ever made.

Quality of a rather different type is to be seen in the wares made at the Weatheriggs pottery near Penrith. Here the kits were all produced in traditional manner with wide-brimmed hoods to the hand-holes and flat-knobbed convex bodies in a dark redware fabric. Instead of using applied clay motifs, the Schofields and Thorburns of Weatheriggs relied exclusively on their superb slip-trailing techniques alone. The earlier kits, such as the 1887 example presented to the City Museum, Stoke-on-Trent by the late Mr M. Schofield (no. 7P52) had their initial slip-trailing executed on the wheel. In this way groups of perfectly parallel and concentric white lines were run round the rim and the upper sections of the body, and the remaining decoration was added when the two sections of the kit had been joined together (see page 107). Such features as sgraffito panels beneath the hand-hole, crude busts down the back of the body and the concentric banding on the wheel all ceased in about the 1920s, the later kits all having the word 'salt' trailed down their fronts. The fluid quality of the vertical bands of pattern still continues, however, the motifs including flowing zig-zags, dots and dashes rapidly applied with a cow-horn and goose-quill trailer.

## *Storage Jars*

The hard, glossy and impervious glazed surface of pottery made it the ideal material for storage jars, for it was extremely light and durable, absolutely airtight and could be readily sterilised by boiling in water. From at least the late seventeenth century pottery jars were extensively used for preserving all manner of fruits, meat and pickles, so that the term 'potted' has come to be almost synonymous with 'preserved' for certain foods, even though they may now be contained in non-ceramic vessels. The earliest preserve jars, often known as 'galleypots' in contemporary recipes, usually held about ½pt, their straight-sided bodies expanding slowly from a fairly narrow base to a flared rim, this being specially shaped to enable the covering material to be securely tied down over it with string. During the eighteenth century the shape was slightly modified, a shoulder being introduced just below the rim to produce the well-known jam-jar shape commonly used up to the time of World War I. Plain jars of this type were made in almost every English country pottery. Decorative jars were also made in certain potteries, these frequently having both the date and their owner's names prominently inscribed round their bodies in white slip, the same techniques often being employed to make finely detailed background patterns.

In Sussex these jars or 'canisters', as they were known here, were usually of an extremely high standard, the potters of Brede probably making most of the finer examples during the late eighteenth and early nineteenth centuries. A number of these appear to have been the work of a single potter, each one being decorated with horizontal bands of interlacing semi-circles formed with a small stamp in the form of a six-pointed star. The Hastings Museum has two pieces of this type inscribed: 'H. RICHARDSON BREDE SEPTEMBER 9 1791' and 'MRS WELLER SEPTEMBER 22 1795' the latter giving a further clue to its origins as the family of Thomas Weller operated the Brede pottery from the 1790s to 1892, when the failure of the claypits forced the works to close down. Other examples made for 'JANE GIBBS HER CANESTER SEPTEMBER 1793' and 'W PAIN 1812' are housed in the collections of the British Museum (no. Q1) and the City of Stoke-on-Trent Museums (no. 41 p47) respectively, thus enabling canisters decorated with this particular pattern to be dated to the period *c.* 1790–1815 with a moderate degree of confidence. The interlacing semi-circle was not the only design to be produced at Brede, however, as is shown by a piece in the Hastings collections, which has the colours reversed, with 'ROBERT MERCER BREDE SUSSEX MARCH 25 1835' inlaid in red lettering on white, while the other takes the form of a beautiful miniature milk churn, the raised bands of which are similar to those seen on the Sussex harvest kegs made here. This was made for 'JANE BUTLER: SEDLESCOMB, SUSSEX: AUGUST.20.1815.', Sedlescombe lying three miles west of the Brede pottery. Storage jars of a fine quality were also made in Yorkshire, those from Halifax frequently having initials, dates and simple quatrefoil motifs inlaid into their red-brown bodies between horizontal bands of white slip, these features being seen on early nineteenth-century pieces in the Halifax Museum's collection. The potters of Burton-in-Lonsdale made their jars cylindrical with domed shoulders and a fairly flat lid, their decoration consisting of carefully trailed scrolls surrounding inscriptions such as: 'Peter & Betty Moore Flookburgh 1819' (Glaisher Collection no. 411).

Besides producing these multi-purpose wares many potters made jars for specific commodities, each one being shaped and decorated according to the user's particular needs. Sugar could most easily be poured into or spooned out of a wide-necked jar. A lid was also useful to keep the sugar clean and dry. In most areas an ordinary jam jar with a bung or paper cover was used, but in north Devon during the late eighteenth century a potter began to make jars specially for this purpose. Each jar was made to contain about 2lb of sugar, and had a close-fitting lid and two small lug handles near the rim. The red fabric was always covered in white slip through which bands of zig-zag decoration were cut, these being identical to those seen on the contemporary north Devon puzzle jugs (see p 112). The most characteristic feature of these jars, however, was their inscriptions, typical ones noted in the collections of the British Museum (no. D120) and the Royal Albert Memorial Museum, Exeter (no. 67/1928.3) advising their owners that

I am But Small for Suger's Dear
of it Be Sure that you take care
Molley Saveall 1791

or that

If you Some Shuger now have Got
Pray put it In this Little pot 1791.

Jars of almost the same shape were made to store honey, too, but as the majority of these are quite plain, they can be attributed to a particular area only through the identification of their materials and techniques. This can prove an extremely difficult process in some cases, for very plain redware pots with unglazed exteriors, such as those made by George Franklin at Leafield in the late nineteenth century, have so few characteristics as to make their certain identification almost impossible (see Oxford City and County Museum, no. 1729). In other areas the potter's individual style is so strong that an attribution may be given without the slightest doubt. In the Royal Albert Memorial Museum at Exeter, for example, there is a large, slightly convex pot (no. 73/1931) decorated in sgraffito with the crude figure of a British lion. The stylistic features clearly indicate that this pot was made by John Bird of Bideford (see pages 76–7) for, as the scroll beneath the lion continues,

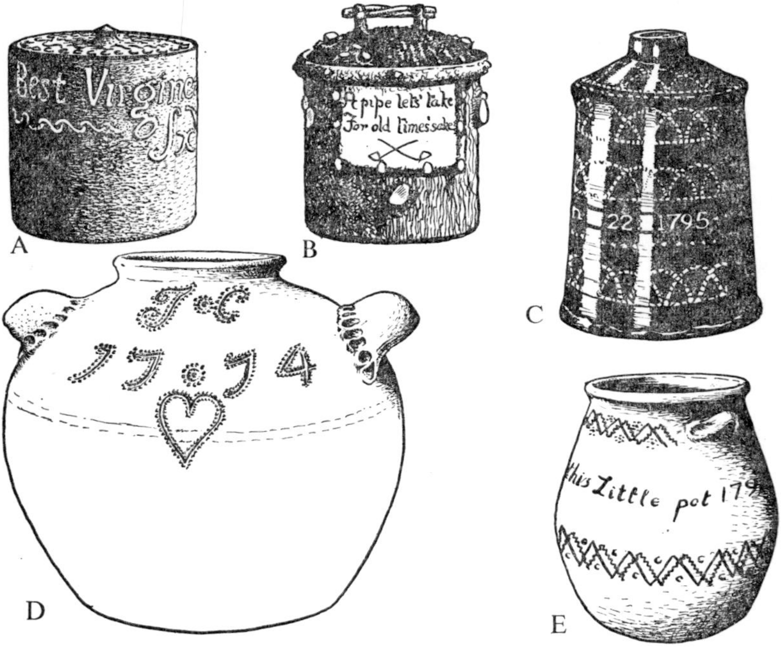


Fig 15 Storage jars made (A) for 'Best Virginea' tobacco at Burton-in-Lonsdale, Yorkshire, in 1823, (B) for tobacco at the Leeds Fireclay Company's Hipperholme Pottery, Halifax, Yorkshire, in the early twentieth century, (C) for tea etc, at Brede, Somerset, in 1895, (D) for nuts in the Farnham area, and (E) for sugar in north Devon in 1791

'Charles Gould June the 10 1807'. Under a small bird at the rear of the pot a further inscription reads:

> Steal not this
> pot for fear of shame
> for here you see
> the owners Name.

Similar problems are frequently associated with tobacco jars too, as, with the exception of a few well-defined types, their identification is also dependent on the clues obtained from their actual materials. Some, like the short cylindrical ones from Burton-in-Lonsdale, complete with their flat, round-knobbed lids, may be recognised immediately by the style and quality of their slip-trailed inscriptions; also, such lines as 'The Best Virginea 1823' (Leicester Museum no. 17A 1856), or 'Robert Hedrington, Hornby. 1865' (Glaisher Collection no. 417) often appear between clay-pipe designs, S-scroll and dot patterns applied in the same technique. At Halifax the order-made pieces of the 1850s and 1860s occasionally copied the shapes of the lead and cast-iron money boxes of that period, adopting a hexagonal form with a matching conical lid. These were among the finest products of the Yorkshire country potteries, their decorations including warm brown mouldings, crossed pipes and masonic emblems inlaid into their cream-buff fabrics, the same clay also being used for the sprig-moulded figures of soldiers etc, which were applied to each face of their polygonal bodies. In the late nineteenth and early twentieth centuries the Leeds Fireclay Company's pottery near Halifax made large numbers of rustic tobacco jars, each one having its brown cylindrical body deeply scored to represent bark, the shallow domed lids being furnished with horizontal bar handles formed from twisted strands of white clay tendril. Almost without exception, these jars have a rectangular compartment of white slip placed just below the rim and the following rhyme, complete with crossed pipes, is cut through it in sgraffito:

A pipe lets take
for old time's sake.

Unlike most other jars these are invariably stamped across their bases with the mark of their makers, 'L.F.C. & CO, HIPPERHOLME'. A limited number of tobacco jars was made early this century by Edwin Beer Fishley of Fremington. Those made by him in 1907 to commemorate the coronation of Edward VII were particularly attractive, standing about 6in high overall. The wide cylindrical jar was sealed by a shallow domed lid, its terminal knob modelled to the form of a miniature crown. Across one side a further crown and the initials 'E.R. 1907' were trailed in relief over the white slipped north Devon fabric, this decoration showing softly through a rich dark-green glaze. Fortunately E. B. Fishley signed almost every piece of his green-glazed wares, thus enabling them to be readily identified.

The storage jars made by the country potter often reached quite large sizes when they were required to hold bulky stores such as bread, flour or nuts. Almost without exception these larger vessels were produced in a coarse redware fabric finished round the interior and rim with a smooth lead glaze. Even though the nature of these materials can often provide evidence for a possible place of manufacture, further clues are to be gained by studying the shapes of the pots themselves, as these tend to vary from one area of the country to another. In the north-western counties bread pots were invariably made in a cylindrical form about 18–24in high by 12–15in in diameter, with two pulled handles at the sides and a flat thrown lid with a central knob. These were still being made by the Schofields and Thorburns of the Weatheriggs Pottery near Penrith to within a few years of World War II. Throughout the remainder of the north and midlands most bread pots took on a rather fuller shape, their bulbous bodies rising from a comparatively narrow base to a wide neck; this neck had either a plain rolled rim, in which case a wooden lid was used, or else one thrown with an internal recess to receive a flat pierced lid of unglazed earthenware. The bread pot of the southern counties was of an entirely different shape, the height of its broad body rarely being greater than its diameter at the rim. The greatest difference, however, was in the design of the lid, for, instead of being a mere disc it rose to form a shallow truncated cone, a single strap handle passing diametrically across its flat top. Pots of this type are still in production at the Harrises' Pottery at Farnham, having been made there since the pottery opened just a hundred years ago.

Large jars for other stores appear to have been made to order in most areas, the potters producing an individual vessel to suit each particular customer's individual requirements. Such pieces with no definite function are to be met with in most parts of the country, and their attributions frequently must rest either on the distinctive features of the fabric and glaze or else on some kind of recorded provenance. A fine example of this type is to be seen in the Curtis Museum at Alton, Hampshire. This is spherical in shape, its unglazed pale orange-red fabric giving it an almost fruit-like appearance. The broad rolled rim round its neck and the two stout handles sliced from a single hemi-spherical bowl of clay demonstrate an admirable sense of design, as these features are in perfect sympathy with the overall shape of the vessel, yet entirely functional in their construction. The decoration, too, is executed in a broad, simple and effective manner, the initials and the date 'J.C. 1774' being cut and stamped into the half-dry surface of the pot with a blunt pointed tool. This jar is known to have been used for the storage of nuts in a farm at East Worldham near Alton up to the 1950s, and so it might well be an early product of the nearby potteries at Farnham, just across the Surrey border.

*Notes for this chapter are on page 179*

## *Chapter Eight*

# *Models*

Most of the country potters working in England found that they had to produce quantities of fairly uniform domestic wares if they were to survive, for these were the mainstay of their craft. A standardisation of the sizes of these vessels was necessary, too, for wares of different heights and diameters would not stack easily in the kiln and would waste space and fuel. If a potter had sufficient time and skill to produce one-off pieces for his own amusement or for a particular customer's individual order he could usually find the opportunity to do so, however. In this way some extremely beautiful examples of ceramic art came into being. Some of the models were made specifically for ceremonial occasions, miniature cradles probably taking a part at christenings or weddings, for example. Others, such as watch-pockets and whistles, were made chiefly as chimney ornaments, while there can be little doubt that many were made purely for the potter's own pleasure, as is illustrated by the examples which have remained in potting families for generation after generation without ever being sold.

One of the most interesting and prolific potters to make these wares was George Fishley of Fremington. He was fortunate enough to have two sons and a grandson working in his pottery during the closing decades of his life and so, being relieved of the necessity of operating the entire business himself, he was left free to model and decorate as he pleased. Ornate chimney ornaments similar to the commercially produced Staffordshire 'flat-backs' formed one of his regular lines, each one being made from a vertical slab of clay about 8in in height with a deep base extending to the front for stability. Having constructed this simple basic shape, he then proceeded to cover its entire face with a mass of ornament in white, mid-brown and manganese-stained dark-brown clays applied over his plain north Devon fabric. His usual motifs, including bunches of grapes, rosettes, female masks and figures of Napoleon (always placed to the left) and a Turk (always placed to the right), were all sprig-moulded from intaglios of his own making, but round these he modelled freehand leaves and pellets, frequently adding three-dimensional fruit, cups, cannons, lambs, dogs, cows or birds along the flat area across the top of the base. Often he would cut a small circular hole through the centre of the ornament to reveal the dial of a watch, a small clay pocket being provided behind to hold the mechanism safely in place. Almost without exception these pieces are all stamped 'G. FISHLEY' 'FREMINGTON' in roman capitals along the front faces of their bases, thus confirming their origins beyond all doubt. Only two bear dates, 1848 and 1849 respectively.[1] It is unlikely that all George Fishley's chimney ornaments were made within this brief two-year period, for he had a long working life and may easily have been making them from the 1840s to the time of his death in 1865.

This suggestion is strengthened by a piece in the Salford Museum's collection. This is a tall Nelson's column, clearly inspired by the one in Trafalgar Square built by William Railton in 1840. It was presumably made shortly after this date, while the news of the column was still fresh in the minds of the sea-going inhabitants of the north Devon coast. At the head of the column stands the figure of Nelson himself, wearing an open coat over his many-buttoned uniform. This is moulded in the typical north Devon fabric, but has such details as his epaulettes and the cockade of his bicorn hat carefully added in white clay. At his feet lie an anchor and a coil of rope, but here the similarities with the Trafalgar Square monument end, for instead of a smooth classical column rising from an elegant square plinth, George Fishley's is enriched with a wealth of detail applied in and above a deep circular base. A small figure, perhaps Napoleon, stands amid grapes, leaves and lambs on a projecting ledge at the foot of the

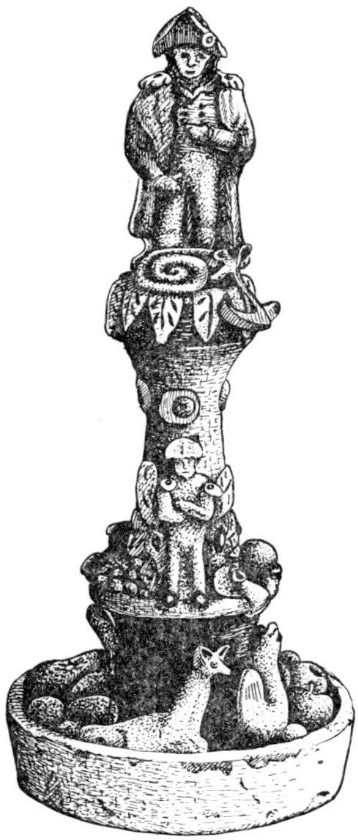

Fig 16 Nelson column by George Fishley of Fremington

column, while below, within a deep basal moulding, sit a hen and a sharp-nosed dog among an abundance of figs, apples, plums and grapes. As an architectural model the column fails miserably, but what it lacks in classical beauty it makes up in sheer exuberance. The piece is full of life, and has the fresh quality of a drawing in which all the essentials have been skilfully noted down without recourse to any tedious detail.

Similar qualities are to be found in most of George Fishley's models, although some of his smaller single figures show that he occasionally followed the designs of mass-produced products very closely. This is seen particularly in his portrait busts of John Wesley,[2] which are copied directly from those of early nineteenth-century Staffordshire, while some of his square-based figures of animals reclining against trees owe much to John Walton of Burslem. These pieces are in a minority, however, as almost all his works are executed entirely in his own inimitable style, for example his clock in the Greg Collection at Manchester (see page 126).

In addition to the Fishleys, the west of England also produced another potter capable of making good quality earthenware figures. A number of museum collections house pieces of a distinctive type, the similarity of their materials and modelling suggesting that they were all the work of a single potter. The main features of this type include the use of warm brown fabrics identical to those of north Devon, the use of a pale-yellow lead glaze over the entire surface and the lack of any moulded details, each piece being built up by hand from slabs or rolls of clay. Subjects include figures of cobblers with their lasts and tools (private collection), men sitting with their dogs (Glaisher Collection no. 349 and Weston Park Museum, Sheffield, no. K 1918.27), women sitting with their pudding-bowls in their laps (Glaisher Collection no. 350), and even Samson wrestling with a lion (Victoria and Albert Museum no. C216.1922). In every case the figures measure about 7in in height and stand on flat rectangular bases. Their modelling is freely executed and is based on acquired knowledge rather than on direct observation. The clothing is generally added on to the basic figure, rather than modelled as an integral part of it. Coats and mufflers are applied as thin sheets of clay and smoothed into union with the clay-rod arms and necks. Some details, including the clay and the dot-textured areas found on these figures, at first suggest that they might have been made by Edwin Beer Fishley of Fremington. Similar materials and textures can be seen on his puzzle jugs, for example (see page 115), but the style of the modelling and the lack of any moulded or contrasting clays and slips make this extremely unlikely, and so a new source has to be found elsewhere. The most convincing evidence of their history exists in the form of a pair of lions housed in the Glaisher Collection at Cambridge (no. 182). Their materials and modelling are identical to those found on the pieces described above (see page 143) but most interesting of all, each one has the name *'H. Davies'* incised across the front of its base, this being accompanied in one case by the words *'Pill Pottery'*. It would therefore appear that H. Davies of Pill, near Bristol, made these figures during the early to mid-nineteenth century. Perhaps he was responsible for the fine model cottage also in the Glaisher Collection (no. 438). This is a small gabled structure with a front porch, a steeply-sloping roof and a tall chimney. Across its gable end runs the incised inscription 'P A 1725', but its rather romantic appearance, with its arched and mullioned windows, its heart-shaped gable aperture and its projecting dormer windows, indicates a later date. It is far more likely to have been made either as a toy, as a pastille burner or as an 'antique' during the middle of the nineteenth century, when such pieces were in great demand.

Further sources of pottery figures also existed in nineteenth-century Sussex, but these are easily identified by their iron-specked Wealden clays and their distinctive shapes. At Brede the potters specialised in life-sized hedgehogs with long smooth snouts, short clawed paws and high-domed backs textured with hundreds of shallow indentations to represent spines. These attractive hedgehogs would probably have been made as presents for children. The other Sussex speciality, the pig, was made for a more useful purpose for, as Llewellynn Jewitt informs us: 'The body, when filled with ale, stands on end, on its tail, and the head lifts off to be used as a drinking cup. ... In Sussex these "pigs" are used at weddings, when each guest is invited to "drink a *hogshead* of beer to the health of the bride"; and at other social and convivial meetings. On these occasions each person is expected to drink this cup—or "hog's head"—full of liquor.'[3] These pigs, each measuring about 11in in overall length, were made exclusively at the

Cadborough and Belle Vue potteries in Rye from the 1860s at least, but their design altered in minor details during the latter years of the nineteenth century. The earlier ones were

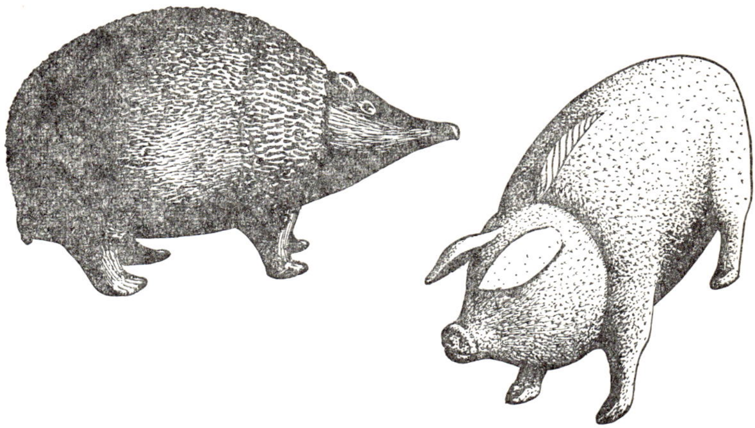

Fig 17 Sussex models of the mid-nineteenth century, the hedgehog from Brede and the pig from Rye

made in the red-firing Wealden clay, while the later ones had a paler fabric heavily speckled with a darker brown colour which bled out into the glaze (see Stoke-on-Trent City Museum no. 4312). Also, as Charles Dawson wrote, the older pigs had heads which

> ... when standing as a cup, rests on the broad snout only, while in the modern one the ears are slightly prolonged to touch the ground for additional safety. The fastening of the head to the body was in the old days by means of a string passed through eyelets in the head and body sections of the figure. Rather later a wooden peg was used to secure the two pieces and the modern ones have a special flange formed in the pottery in the head of the pig, which looks into an eyelet perforated in the lid-flange of the body section.[4]

In the northern counties the potters made very few figures of either men or animals but, with the exception of an excellent range of bird-calls, they concentrated their modelling skills into the making of miniature pieces of furniture. Unfortunately there are no records as to why these were made. Matching rocking chair and cradle sets bearing the same date are known, suggesting that they were made to commemorate a particular event such as a christening or wedding, but one of the only fully provenanced examples of this type of furniture was made as a toy by a potter's child.

Chests of drawers form some of the most interesting wares of this type, the finest ones being made at the Woodman House Pottery near Halifax. Recently a member of the potter's family presented some of her ancestor's wares to the Folk Museum of West Yorkshire at Shibden Hall, Halifax, and these included a fine chest of drawers money box made by Elizabeth Kitson when working in her father's pottery (see page 62). The materials and workmanship of these pieces display a very distinctive style which enables other products of this pottery to be identified fairly easily. In every case the basic construction of the piece is carried out in the usual red-firing coal-measure clay which can range from a pale-brown colour to a near-black beneath its lead glaze, the actual tone depending solely on the temperature to which it was fired. A creamy-white fabric is applied over this in the form of long strips about a $\frac{1}{4}$in wide by up to $\frac{1}{8}$in in thickness, V-shaped notches being either rouletted or stamped into these at regular intervals along their length. Most Woodman House chests of drawers stand approximately 6in in height on either four or six slightly conical feet, and have a symmetrical frontage with two drawers set to the left and to the right of a central arch-topped cupboard. The drawers which survive intact slide smoothly into flat-bottomed housings within the body, a border of white clay round the face of each one helping to disguise any irregularities in the joints. Beyond these general characteristics the Woodman House potters employed a variety of decorative features, no two chests of drawers being finished in exactly the same manner. One in the City Museum, Stoke-on-Trent, has flying birds applied across its top and sides in notched strips of white clay, while another in the Glaisher

Collection (no. 408) has the figures of two long-skirted ladies wearing bonnets rising above its slip-trailed front (see page 144). This was the only pottery to make chests of drawers in Yorkshire, but others were produced in the Tyne Valley round Newcastle. No fully provenanced examples have yet been recorded from this area, but the North of England Open Air Museum at Beamish Park possesses a magnificent specimen in a dark-red clay and creamy-white slip identical to that used in making the traditional Newcastle baking dishes. Its walls are far thinner and flatter than in those from Yorkshire, and its drawer fronts extend slightly beyond the edges of the drawers themselves so as to mask the recesses in the carcase entirely. The quality of the slip trailing is far better too, for instead of the rather irregular patterning seen on page 144, the sides, top and drawer front panels are neatly filled with wavy line or dot motifs running between pairs of beautifully straight lines to give a particularly bright and fresh appearance.

The potters of Newcastle and Halifax were also responsible for the production of small rocking chair ornaments, examples made in the local redware fabrics still being found near these towns. The chairs are closely modelled on the plank-built children's chairs of oak or ash made up to about 1900 in the north. Their sides are always cut to a projecting winged design, while the back is invariably brought to an interesting curved outline (see page 144).

The custom of making miniature cradles first became popular in the mid-seventeenth-century slipware potteries of north Staffordshire; examples measured between 6in and 16in in length and were made in a variety of designs. Most cradles of this period are modelled on contemporary oak originals, with fairly long bodies mounted on shallow rockers. Their footboards and hoods rise up to curved, gabled or square outlines at opposite ends of their box-like bodies, while small knobs usually extend from their sides and upper edges to enable a muslin cat-cover to be secured over their open tops. Motifs including the monarch's head, scrolls and abstract floral patterns are frequently trailed round their exteriors, the finer ones also having their dates and owners' names boldly added in jewelled slip. Others are elaborately decorated with applied clay figures, and one exceptional example of this type in the Robert Hall Warren Collection at the Ashmolean Museum, Oxford, has four white Aaron Wood-style heads added to the corners of its curving hood. A lively fiddler sits gaily on top of this cradle, probably representing the musician employed to entertain the wedding or christening party. Few of these early cradles can be attributed to a definite maker for, though the trailing on some of them is identical to that found on plates of the same date, showing that the same potters were making both types of vessel,[5] many years of patient research are still required before they can be identified with any degree of certainty.

From a stylistic study it can be seen that cradles were still being made in the Staffordshire potteries up to the late eighteenth century, but it is not until 1839 that the first fully provenanced example emerges from this century. In 1945 the City of Stoke-on-Trent Museums purchased a cradle (no. 637P45) made at Little London near Willenhall by Fred Wootton, the vendor's great uncle. Surprisingly little of the early Staffordshire potter's skills are to be seen here, for the cradle (see figure 18) is rather heavy and coarse in its construction. Instead of the smooth, fine, and regular edges usually found in seventeenth-century cradles, this one has them cut with a knife or a wire to a stout zig-zag profile. The cat-cover knobs are omitted completely in preference to two small handles of twisted clay, while the decoration has degenerated into plain rows of dark brown slip S-scrolls trailed over a deep buff fabric. By 1839, when this cradle was made, the Staffordshire slipwares were approaching their final decline, and it is to the Yorkshire potters that we must look to discover good quality cradles at this date.

In the Halifax area there were two major families producing earthenware cradles during the nineteenth century: the Hallidays of Howcans and the Kitsons of Woodman House.

The former potters, resident here from at least the 1640s, were already making excellent cradles by 1802, as may be seen from a dated example in the Yorkshire Museum at York (no.

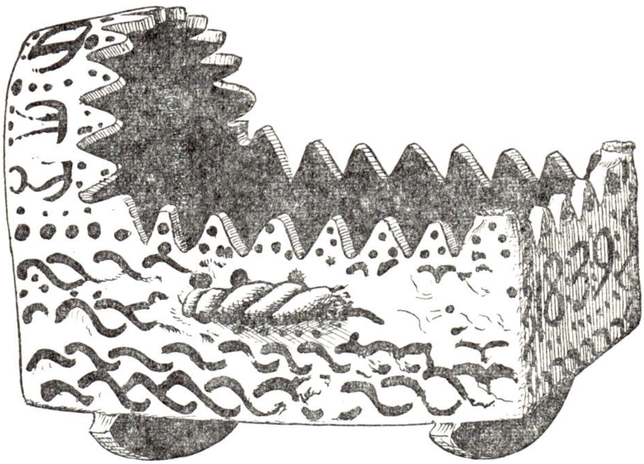

Fig 18 Cradle made by Fred Wootton at Little London, near Willenhall, Staffordshire, in 1839

73/a). These early cradles are made from very thin sheets of red-firing clay, with deep rectangular bodies covered at one end by a simple semi-cylindrical hood. A pair of knobs on each side and an undulating border of white clay applied to the upper edges form their only three-dimensional embellishments, but the addition of a date, a floral motif and a wavy line-and-dot frieze in white slip transform these plain pieces. The red and white clays do not contrast harshly as in some Halifax products, but instead their deep-yellow lead glaze mellows them to glowing warm-brown tones which add greatly to their beauty. By the 1870s the Howcans cradles had altered greatly in style, their early simplicity being replaced by more precise and accurately observed modelling. They were made in the manner of wood, slices of leather-hard agate ware being cut to shape and stuck together with slip just as the joiner would use planks of wood and glue. Even the mouldings across the top of the canopy and all round the base are reproduced exactly, while an example of this later type in the Yorkshire Museum (no. 74/a) has its rockers marked 'F' and 'H. 1876' for its foot and head respectively.

This mechanical quality is entirely absent from the work of the Kitsons of Woodman House. Their cradles all have long narrow bodies tapering a little towards the base, while their hoods are formed from short cylindrical vessels thrown on the wheel. As with all the finer Kitson pieces, the decoration is executed with white clay motifs applied over a normal red-ware fabric, the quality and quantity of this varying greatly from one piece to another. One of the cradles presented to the Folk Museum of West Yorkshire at Shibden Hall, Halifax, by a member of the Kitson family is extremely plain (see page 144). Only the knobs and the simple details across the hood are added in white, though the typical V-roulette has been run round the edge of the body. A second Kitson cradle in the same collection is much richer, for the potters have added large vertical scrolls at the junction of the body and the canopy, while the body itself bears a rouletted border of white clay beneath which runs the inscription 'F.R.B. 1835' in the same material.[6]

The whistles made by the country potters may readily be divided into two main classes, the first consisting of the small plain whistles given away to potential purchasers' children in order to attract their parents' custom, while the second is made up of ornate whistles and bird-calls designed to grace the mantle-shelf or window-sill of the cottage. Of the former group very few examples survive, for they were easily broken or lost by their young owners. The Yorkshire Museum has one in agate ware which measures just over 1in in length, this probably being made by Jonathan Catherall of the Soil Hill Pottery in Halifax. He attributed his success as a potter to the extensive trade he had built up through a preliminary distribution of such toys round the area he served, even going so far as to christen his house 'Whistle Hall' in commemoration of the event.

The larger whistles and bird-calls are far more interesting, for because of their modelling and the pride taken in their ownership they have survived in much greater numbers. The most common variety is made in a brick-red fabric and is formed as a large cuckoo perched on a horizontal branch mounted at the tip of a tall conical base (see figure 19). Both

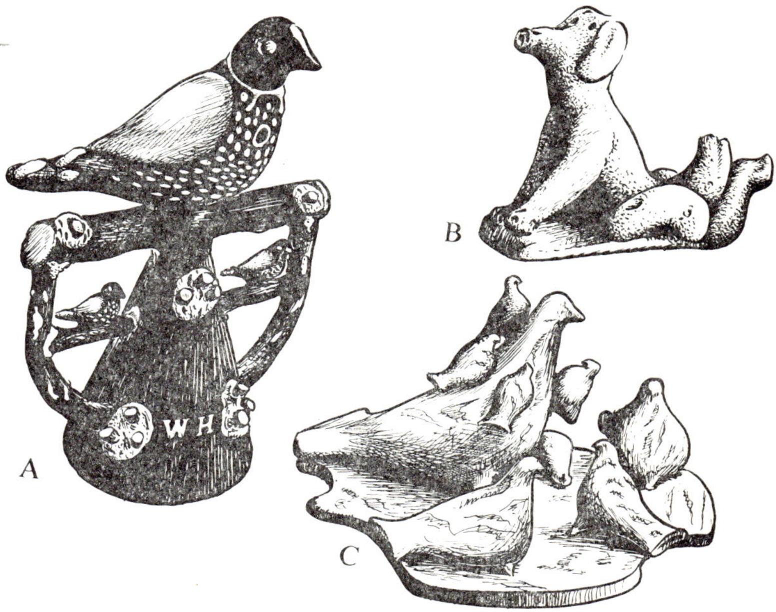


A B C

Fig 19 Whistles made in (A) nineteenth-century Yorkshire, (B) north Devon and (C) Sussex

the branch and the base bear gnarled knots of applied clay, the three or more sawn-off shoots extending from these being tipped with white slip. Usually a small cuckoo is added to each side of the base and, on the better pieces, an extra curving branch arches completely over the central bird, further miniature cuckoos and knots being applied along it to complete a particularly pleasing design measuring about 10in high. These pieces are capable of producing a very realistic cuckoo-call, the two notes being made by blowing up a slot in the tip of the tail and alternately covering and opening a hole pierced through the hollow chest. Various attributions have been given to this group of whistles, some authorities claiming them for Sussex, while others have favoured Cockpit Hill, Derbyshire, or even Staffordshire. The former suggestion appears to be correct, for although their fabrics do contain a few minute specks of iron, the presence of numerous white to yellow particles resting on the surface of the ware beneath the glaze confirms their northern coal-measure origins. One or two examples are made in a buff fabric glazed with a yellow-tinted lead glaze coarsely splashed with manganese to produce an almost tortoiseshell finish.[7] This type of ware occurs only in Yorkshire, and so it is most likely that they were made in that county. Further clues may be obtained from their methods of decoration. Their slip-trailed beaks, eyes, chest-dots and plain wings could have been executed at any Yorkshire pottery, but the white initials inlaid into the base with printer's type (including 'TN' in the British Museum no. D83a) and 'ET' in the Burnap Collection, Kansas (no. 64), can have been made only at a limited number of sites. As the potters of both Burton-in-Lonsdale and Woodman House, Halifax, are known to have type-impressed many of their stonewares, and as they also made earthenware pieces featuring decorative birds and rustic motifs, they are the most likely makers; but as Oxley Grabham reported that cuckoos were being made by the Catheralls of Soil Hill, Halifax, it is uncertain as to which of these Yorkshire potteries these cuckoo-calls should be attributed.

Other bird-calls were also made in Sussex, but these are easily identified from the pale colour and fine grain of their agate-ware fabrics. Most of them consist of single birds mounted on short conical bases, the whole piece measuring only about 3in in height. Others were made in more complex forms with small flocks of birds of different sizes perching round the perimeter of a flat-shaped base. One of these in the Glaisher Collection (no. 435, see figure 19) bears four major birds, their flat splayed tails overhanging the edge of the base to serve as mouthpieces for the whistles concealed inside their hollow bodies. The rarest Sussex whistles are much larger. Edmund Austen of Brede acquired a fine redware example inlaid with white feather designs which had been discovered when demolishing the chimney of Court Lodge, Udimore. According to Mr Austen: 'These birds were made with a whistle in the tail. They were often built into old farmhouse chimneys, so that when the wind blew, the bird whistled, which was thought to keep evil spirits away—a symbolic survival of the rites of long ago.' It is difficult to imagine how a device of this type could function inside a large smoking chimney, but as the writer was an authority on Sussex folklore, his word must be accepted.

Very few whistles or bird-calls were made elsewhere in England, but occasional pieces are found with fabrics which reveal unexpected sources. None is recorded in the literature concerning the potteries of the south west for example, but a whistle in the collections at Kirkstall Abbey House, Leeds, shows by its style and materials that it was undoubtedly made in the nineteenth century by one of the north Devon potters. It takes the form of a small dog sitting alert on a low flat base which houses the whistle itself (see figure 19). It is an extremely simple piece of modelling, the basic shapes being made up from short rolls of clay rapidly stroked and squeezed together to present an appealing canine portrait which any child would be proud to possess.

*Notes for this chapter are on pages 179–80*

# *Notes in the Text*

INTRODUCTION (pages 9–12)

1 Llorens Artigas & Corredor-Matheos. *Spanish Folk Ceramics* (1970)

*1* THE DEVELOPMENT OF THE CRAFT (pages 13–30)

1 Brears, P. C. D. *The English Country Pottery, Its History and Techniques* (1971), 18–23

2 Plot, R. *Natural History of Staffordshire* (1686)

3 Kinder, P. *Collections towards a History of Derbyshire* (*c.* 1650); manuscript in the Bodleian Library, Oxford

4 Barton, K. J. 'The Excavation of a Medieval Bastion at St Nicholas's Almshouses, King Street, Bristol', *Medieval Archaeology*, 8(1964), 202–7

5 Brears, P. C. D. 'Excavations at Potovens', *Post Medieval Archaeology*, 1 (1967), 16

6 Brears, P. C. D. *The Farnham Potteries* (1971)

7 Burnet, J. *Plenty and Want*, Pelican edn (1968), 20

8 Levi, L. 'Wages and Earnings of the Working Classes', Report to Sir Arthur Bliss, MP (1885), 30

9 These were the potteries of W. F. Harris & Sons, Farnham Pottery, Wrecclesham, Farnham, Surrey, and that of the Lakes, Truro Pottery, Chapel Hill, Truro, Cornwall

*2* MATERIALS AND TECHNIQUES (pages 31–55)

1 When an early post-medieval kiln was recently excavated at Lakes's Pottery, Truro, the unglazed sherds were all of this micacious nature.

2 Brears, P. C. D. *The English Country Pottery, Its History and Techniques* (1971) 71 and 112; and Watkins, C. M. 'North Devon Pottery and its Export to America in the Seventeenth Century', *United States National Museum Bulletin*, 225 (Washington 1960)

3 Coleman-Smith, R. and Pearson, T. *Excavations at Donyatt and Nether Stowey, Somerset* (Southampton 1970), 2
4 Demonstrated to the author by Mr H. Thorburn at the Weatheriggs Pottery, Penrith
5 Holland, W. F. *Fifty Years a Potter* (1958), 13
6 Described to the author by Mr R. Bateson of the Burton-in-Lonsdale potteries
7 An example of this practice is to be seen in the collection of the Hampshire County Museum Service
8 Brears, P. C. D. 'Techniques of the Truro Pottery *Folk Life,* 10 (1972), 47–54

*3* Money Boxes (pages 56–65)
1 Holling, F. W. 'A Preliminary Note on the Pottery Industry of the Hampshire-Surrey Borders', *Surrey Archaeological Collections,* 68 (1971), 80

*4* Harvest Wares (pages 66–93)
1 Jeckyl, G. and Jones, S. R. *Old English Household Life* (1925), 112
2 Wright, J. *The English Dialect Dictionary* (1961 edn)
3 A good example is housed in East Riddlesden Hall, Keighley, Yorkshire
4 Jago, F. W. P. *Glossary of Cornish Dialect* (Truro 1882)
5 For details of the early development of these wares see Watkins, C. M. 'North Devon Pottery and its Export to America in the Seventeenth Century', *United States National Museum Bulletin* 225 (Washington 1960)

*5* Flower Pots (pages 94–105)
1 Emmison, F. *Tudor Food and Pastimes* (1964)
2 Brears, P. C. D. 'Finds from Basing House, Hampshire; The Horticultural Wares', *Post Medieval Archaeology,* 4 (1970), 87–90
3 Douch, H. L. 'Cornish Earthenware Potters', *Journal of the Royal Institution of Cornwall,* New Series, 6, part 1, (1969), 60
4 Walton, J. 'Some Decadent Local Industries: Pottery', *Halifax Antiquarian Society Transactions* (1939), 19
5 Evans, G. E. *Where Beards Wag All* (1970), 215
6 Douch, in *Journal of the Royal Institution of Cornwall,* 34

*6* Jokes and Puzzles (pages 106–22)
1 See the Glaisher Collection, Fitzwilliam Museum, Cambridge,

nos. 25 and 26 (1569 and 1571 respectively) and the Victoria and Albert Museum (Museum of Practical Geology catalogue no. F17)

2 City of Stoke-on-Trent Museum and Art Gallery no. 2765

3 Somerset County Museum, Taunton. Similar rhymes dated 1793 and 1794 are known in the Glaisher Collection, nos. 169 and 172

4 Somerset County Museum, Taunton

5 Glaisher Collection no. 175

6 Leicester City Museum no. 62A.1946

7 City of Stoke-on-Trent Museum and Art Gallery no. 938 P49

8 Glaisher Collection no. 176

9 *Connoisseur,* 41 (1915), 88–92

10 See Hodgkin, J. E. and E. *Examples of Early English Pottery* (1896), no. 4

11–13 Somerset County Museum, Taunton

14 Stoke-on-Trent Museum and Art Gallery no. 599 P44

15 British Museum no. D117

16 London Museum no. A 12178 and Glaisher Collection no. 165

17 The Museum, Lynton, Devon

18 City of Stoke-on-Trent Museum and Art Gallery no. 116 P38

19 British Museum no. D118

20 Somerset County Museum, Taunton

21 Dent, G. in *Connoisseur,* 87 (1931), 309–11

*7* Kitchen and Table (pages 123–61)

1 Cooper, R. G. *English Slipware Dishes 1650–1850* (1968)

2 Kenworthy, J. *The Midhope Potteries* (Sheffield 1928), 87

3 Hodgkin, nos. 131 and 132

4 Kenworthy, 73

5 Pepys's Diary, 16 January, 1667

*8* Models (pages 162–75)

1 The dated watch-pockets are in the Burton Art Gallery, Bideford (no. 276) and the Glaisher Collection in the Fitzwilliam Museum, Cambridge (no. 87). Undated examples are in the Royal Albert Memorial Museum, Exeter (nos. 89/1928.1, 71/1930.1, and 71/1930.2), the Glaisher Collection (no. 88) and the Greg Collection at Manchester City Art Gallery (no. 104 1923.161)

2 Glaisher Collection nos. 92 and 93

3 Jewitt, L. *The Ceramic Art of Great Britain,* 1 (1878), 458

4 Dawson, C. 'Sussex Pottery', *Sussex Archaeological Collections*, 46 (1903), 31

5 Compare the decoration of the bird-motifs on the eighteenth-century cradle in the City of Stoke-on-Trent Museum and Art Gallery's collection with that on the plate in the Lomax Collection illustrated in Cooper, R. G. *English Slipware Dishes 1650–1850* (1968), figure 285

6 Brears, P. C. D. *The English Country Pottery* (1971), 86, shows this cradle, which is now recognised as a Woodman House piece

7 See Weston Park Museum, Sheffield no. K1927.58 and Burnap Collection, Kansas no. 68

# *Notes on the Plates*

HALIFAX CANDLE HOLDER (page 17)
Glaisher Collection no. 400. This redware candle holder forms part of a group made by Samuel Catherall of the Soil Hill Pottery, Halifax during the 1860s and 1870s. The sprig-moulded face mask and ring-and-dot slip trailing are typical features of his work.

WATTISFIELD TILE (page 17)
British Museum no. C41. This redware tile, probably of eighteenth-century date, has been given a decorative raised design by the use of a 1¾in-diameter pastry roller. A label on the rear states: 'Probably from the Pottery at Wattisfield, Suffolk, J. Warren'.

PAINTED POSSET POT (page 18)
Halifax Museums Collection. This vessel has a buff fabric covered with a dark-red slip and a near-black glaze, the final colouring being applied in Venetian red and cream oil colour. Dated 1737, it was probably made at the Bate Hayne Pottery, Halifax.

GORSTY HILL MONEY BOX (page 35)
Victoria and Albert Museum Collection no. C 336–1919. The hen-and-chickens money boxes made at Gorsty Hill, Worcestershire are easily distinguished by their large 'hens' with whistles mounted in their tails. Both white on dark-brown and dark-brown on white slip decorated examples are known.

BURTON-IN-LONSDALE MONEY BOX (page 35)
Private collection. This redware pot was made for James Whitaker, master of the Kendal Bluecoat School 1837–78, by a potter who was given the order while visiting Kendal Fair in 1838. The open lantern in the centre contains a miniature bird. Note the neat lettering trailed between grooves thrown round the body of the box itself.

CHEST OF DRAWERS MONEY BOX (page 36)
Halifax Museums Collection. This piece is made of dark-red, light-red and white agate-ware, except for a plain redware back panel into which is inlaid the following inscription in white: 'LOT. SLADEN.APRIL 27.1846'.

FARNHAM PIG MONEY BOX (page 36)
Private collection. This pig was made *c.* 1890 by William Freemantle Harris of the Farnham Pottery, Surrey. It is press-moulded in a red fabric and has a rich copper-green glaze.

DONYATT PUZZLE JUG (page 53)
Temple Newsam House, Leeds. This jug, decorated with typical Donyatt sgraffito motifs, is one of the earliest dated examples from this pottery, being inscribed 'Fill me full Drink of Me while you woul Mary Roge 1740'.

DONYATT 'JOLLY BOYS' (page 53)
City of Stoke-on-Trent Museum and Art Gallery no. 116 P 38. Decorated with typical Donyatt sgraffito motifs, this late eighteenth-century piece is inscribed 'In your/sight is my/delight'.

BRIDGWATER PUZZLE JUG (page 54)
Glaisher Collection no. 181. This redware jug was made in the Bridgwater pottery of J. Brown & Sons during the late nineteenth century by 'A Nicholls', whose stamp it bears. Note the unusual spring-moulded decoration of a stag, hounds and huntsmen round the body.

HALIFAX FROG MUG (page 54)
Halifax Museums Collection. This redware piece bears the inscription 'Last kiln at Howcans, 1889' in pencil across its base, being made at that pottery for 'Robert and Sarah Knight, Feb. 9, 1886 I.L.1889'.

DORSET PILL (page 71)
Private collection. Pills or 'owls' of this type were made in a number of potteries in the Verwood area up to the 1950s. All have the same general shape and a coarse buff fabric half covered in a thin yellow glaze.

SUSSEX FLASKS (page 71)
Victoria and Albert Museum Collection no. C 349–1919 (left)

was made by John Siggery of the Boship Pottery, Lower Dicker, in 1794. Its sides read:

| | |
|---|---|
| Otions of Brandy<br>And Rivers of Wine<br>Plantecion of Tea & a garle<br>To my mind 1794 | OF a Little Take a Little<br>Your Welcome Thare unto<br>But of a Little Leave a Little<br>Tis Manners So To Do<br>William Miller<br>1794 |

No. C 574–1925, probably made at Chailey, is dated 'JANUARY 17 1797'.

North Devon Jug by Edward Reed (page 72)

City of Stoke-on-Trent Museum and Art Gallery no. 304 P 40. This magnificent jug is described in detail on page 76.

North Devon Jug by Robert Fishley (page 72)

City of Stoke-on-Trent Museum and Art Gallery no. 322 P 50. This jug, made at Fremington in 1834, is described on page 80. Note the leaf-resist pattern round the neck.

North Devon Jug by John Hoyle (page 89)

Glaisher Collection no. 75. This jug is described on page 84.

North Devon Jug by John Phillips (page 89)

North Devon Athenaeum, Barnstaple. This jug is described on page 85.

Lantern (page 90)

Public Library and Museum, Whitehaven. This lantern/candlestick was produced by John Kitchin of the Ginns Pottery, Whitehaven in the 1850s, and is made from a dark-red, light-red and white agate-ware fabric with details applied in white clay.

Flower Pot Holders (page 90)

Halifax Museums Collection. Both were probably made by Samuel Catherall at the Soil Hill Pottery, Halifax, during the 1850s (see page 102).

Woodman House Salt Kit (page 107)

Collection of Mr J. de Kleyn. This unique redware piece is easily recognised as a Woodman House piece from the V-notched strips of clay applied round its sides. The fine rolls of clay in the cartouche beneath the hand-hole reads 'D + E 1847'.

WEATHERIGGS SALT KIT (page 107)

City of Stoke-on-Trent Museum and Art Gallery no. 7 P 52. This redware kit was presented to the museum by Mr M. Schofield of the Weatheriggs pottery, where it had been made in 1887. Clifton is the hamlet near Penrith in which the pottery is situated.

HONEY JAR BY JOHN BIRD (page 108)

Royal Albert Memorial Museum, Exeter, no. 73/1931. This jar, made in Bideford in 1807, shows all the characteristics of John Bird's work. The lion's teeth, tail, eyes and crown are particularly distinctive. It is inscribed: 'Steal not this pot for fear of shame for here you see the owners Name', and 'Charles Gould June the 10 1807'.

HOWCANS CUTLERY BOX (page 108)

Halifax Museums Collection. This is one of the finest nineteenth-century cutlery boxes to have been made at the Howcans Pottery, Halifax, its white clay designs being inlaid into the red fabric with great skill. It is dated '8 February 3 1853' across the handle.

POLESWORTH DISH (page 125)

Birmingham City Art Gallery no. M 100.70. This dish was recently discovered during ploughing at Polesworth, Warwickshire. As its materials are identical to those of a jug marked 'Polesworth Pottery 1800' in the Glaisher Collection at Cambridge (no. 365) it is presumably a Polesworth piece.

TYNESIDE DISH (page 125)

Private collection. These red-fabric pressed-ware dishes, decorated with sprays of white slip dashes, were made in the Newcastle area from at least the early nineteenth century. They are to be found in most parts of the country (but particularly in the eastern counties) as they were frequently carried by coastal vessels engaged in the coal trade.

WATCH-POCKET BY GEORGE FISHLEY (page 126)

Manchester City Art Gallery no 1923–194 Greg 137. This watch-pocket is one of George Fishley's finest works. Made at Fremington, north Devon, in the mid-nineteenth century, it demonstrates both his lively modelling and his inventive skill.

LIONS BY H. DAVIES (page 143)

Glaisher Collection no. 182. These lions, incised 'H. Davies.

Pill Pottery' and 'H. Davies' respectively, were made at Pill, near Bristol, during the early-to-mid-nineteenth century. They form part of a group of his wares described on page 166.

Model Cottage (page 143)
Glaisher Collection no. 438. Although inscribed 'P A 1725' across the gable, this model was probably made by H. Davies of the Pill Pottery near Bristol during the early-to-mid-nineteenth century. The interior is fitted with a fireplace and may have served as a pastille burner, as a toy or as a falsely dated 'antique'.

Rocking Chair (page 144)
Halifax Museums Collection. This redware chair, dated 1871 in white slip, could have been made in a number of Halifax potteries.

Halifax Cradle (page 144)
Halifax Museums Collection. This piece was presented to the museum by a member of the Kitson family, who stated that it had been made at her ancestor's Woodman House Pottery near Halifax about the middle of the nineteenth century. Note the V-notched strip round the centre of its body.

Chest of Drawers (page 144)
Glaisher Collection no. 408. This redware chest of drawers shows a number of features associated with the Kitsons of Woodman House Pottery near Halifax. These include the V-notching of the drawer fronts, the arrangement of the drawers, the bun-shaped feet and the applied figures at each end of the top. It probably dates from the mid-nineteenth century.

# *Glossary*

The names of the different types of pottery vessel, and those of the numerous methods of making and decorating, vary considerably from one area of England to another. A plain redware jug, for example, may be a gotch, a gullymouth, a long tom, a pinchgut, a pitcher or a thirtytale, depending upon its size and the local dialect term. Similarly a piece of pottery made from a mixture of two clays of different colours may be variously described as an example of agate ware, grained ware or snail-horn ware.

In this glossary, therefore, the various terms have been gathered together and classified to avoid further confusion. In most cases the terms have been recorded from the potters themselves by the author, but where a written source has been consulted also, its bibliographical reference has been included.

| | |
|---|---|
| AGATE WARE | See *Ware* |
| APPLE ROASTER | See *Ovens* |
| BAKER | A Cornish term for a shallow dish used for baking. In use a wood fire was lit on top of a flat stone, and allowed to burn clear. The ashes were then pushed to one side and the food, covered by the baker, placed on the slab. The baker was then covered with the hot ashes and fresh turfs and so remained until the food was finally cooked. This technique was used in Cornwall up to the late nineteenth century (see *Medieval Archaeology*, 6 [1962], 290) |
| BAKING DISH | A shallow pressed-ware dish, often decorated with trailed slip, used for general baking purposes from the early eighteenth century |
| BARM POT | A pot for holding yeast. It is normally a tall cylindrical jar with a rolled rim over which a paper cover can be tied |
| BEDPANS | Redware bedpans, copying pewter originals, |

have a shallow bowl, perhaps 12in in diameter and 3in in depth, with a wide inturned rim seat. From one side projects a wide tubular handle/urinal/cleaning spout. Made from early nineteenth century at least

BISCUIT — Unglazed fired ware

BLACKWARE — See *Ware*

BLISTER OR BLOATING — The swelling or bubble occasionally formed within the fabric or glaze of a pot while it is in the kiln, formed by gases originating from impurities such as lime

BOBS — The small clay pellets on which pots are stood during the glaze firing to prevent their sticking to the saggers. 'Bobbs' are mentioned in Dr Plot's *History of Staffordshire* of 1686

BODY 1. The main section of a pot

2. The potter's name for the substance of which the pot is made. In this volume it is replaced by the term 'fabric', as used by the collector and the archaeologist, to avoid any ambiguity

BOWING — A north Devon term for applying the handles

BOWL — An open vessel with shaped sides (ie not a pancheon)

BROWNWARE — See *Ware*

BUNG-HOLE POT — A large pottery cistern equipped with a spiggot hole at the base. Used to dispense small quantities of liquid for domestic purposes in northern England from the fifteenth to the late nineteenth century

BUSSA — A variety of pan used for pickling pilchards in Devon and Cornwall

BUTTER POT 1. A tall cylindrical unglazed pot made in Burslem, Staffordshire for the storage of butter for sale. By Act of Parliament 13 and 14 (Chas. II, cap. 26 [1661]), these pots were to weigh less than 6lb but contain 14lb of butter; they must not be so porous as to imbibe much water, which could be counted in the weight of the butter

2. A tall cylindrical pot used from the eighteenth to the twentieth century for salting down butter for domestic use

CAUDLE POT — A pot for serving caudle, an oatmeal gruel enriched with spices and wine. It is shaped like an oversized mug with two opposed handles, although multi-handled examples are known

CAWDERN — See *Pan*

CHAD-POT — A Buckinghamshire term for a fire-pot (see Wright, Thomas. *The Romance of the Lace Pillow* 1919)

CHAFING DISH — A shallow bowl-shaped vessel mounted on a tall pedestal base and having a number of knobs or spikes projecting from its upper rim on which a secondary food bowl may be placed. In use, the bowl of the dish is filled with burning charcoal, which gives sufficient heat to cook or warm the food above when at table

CHARGER — A large shallow plate

CHICKEN FEEDER — Pots made in a variety of designs, all having a hopper arrangement by which chickens can feed themselves from a self-filling grain trough

CHILL — A Cornish pottery lamp having a shallow bowl in which train oil is burnt from a wick

CHURN — A pottery version of the wooden plunger-churn, usually made in the nineteenth century with a ceramic body and lid and a wooden plunger

CLOAM — A Devon and Cornwall term for earthenware in general

CLOAMER'S BOYS — Cornish clay marbles

CLOUGH — A meat-salting pan (see Morton's *Natural History of Northamptonshire,* 1712)

CLOUT — A Derbyshire term for a large brown-glazed mug

COCKSPURS — See *Spurs*

COILING — The process of building up a pot with successive rolls of clay placed one upon the other and smoothed together. This technique was never used commercially, being much slower and vastly inferior to throwing

COMBING — A technique of slip decoration in which a dipped pot is decorated with a blunt-toothed comb of wood, bone or leather, thus exposing the colour of the fabric beneath

COSTREL — A squat bottle with two pierced lugs for suspension at the shoulder

CRAZING — The fine network of cracks often found in the glaze of a pot

| | |
|---|---|
| CREAM POT | A pot of 3–4gal capacity used to hold cream |
| DAFFER | A Cornish term for crockery such as tea things (see Jago, F. W. P. *Glossary of Cornish Dialect* [Truro 1882]) |
| DICKY POT | A Bedfordshire term for a fire pot |
| DIPPING | The method of applying either slip or glaze to a pot by immersing it in the particular solution required |
| DUTCH OVEN | See *Oven* |
| EARTHENWARE | See *Ware* |
| FABRIC | The substance of which the pot is made |
| FEATHERING | A method of slip decoration in which different colours of wet slip are drawn one into the other over the surface of a pot by the use of a fine point such as the tip of a feather |
| FIRECLAY | A coarse yellow or grey clay having the property of withstanding very high temperatures without deforming |
| FIREDOG | Earthenware firedogs for use in the domestic hearth were made in the seventeenth-century Barnstaple potteries |
| FIRE-POT | A pot shaped rather like a chamber pot with small holes pierced through its walls near its rim. It was filled with hot ashes and placed beneath the skirts of lacemakers and others to give them 'central heating' |
| FISH DISH | A shallow leaf-shaped dish about 15in long and 3in deep, usually having a handle projecting from one side and a spout at each end |
| FLAKING | The peeling or scaling of slips or glazes from a fabric due to their unsuitable composition, the action of frost or their prolonged contact with salt |
| FLATWARE | Any broad shallow ware such as plates, saucers or shallow bowls |
| FOUNTAIN | A pot with an air-lock arrangement which automatically refills an animal's water-trough as it drinks |
| FROG MUG | A drinking mug, usually made between the eighteenth and twentieth centuries, which has a frog realistically modelled within it so as to emerge as the liquid is drunk |
| FUDDLING CUP | A trick cup with a number of chambers linked |

| | |
|---|---|
| | by internal tubes, from which the drinker has to discover a method of drinking without being drenched |
| FUMING POT | A bowl-shaped vessel standing on a tall pedestal base and having its upper section pierced to produce an open lantern-like top. These pots, termed 'stink pots' during the Great Plague, were probably used to hold some form of pot-pourri to scent the rooms (see Bell, W. G. *The Great Plague in London 1665,* 2nd edn, [1951], 106, 155 and 285, and *Surrey Arch. Coll.,* 58 [1961], 17) |
| GALENA | A raw lead ore, chiefly lead sulphide, used as a glaze |
| GALLIPOT 1. | A small pot used to contain medicines or preserves, with a rolled rim over which a paper cover can be tied |
| 2. | A paint pot in north Devon |
| GOTCH | An East Anglian term for a jug |
| GRAINED WARE | A Westmorland term for agate-ware; see *Ware* |
| GREATCROCK | A large pot used for pickling pilchards in north Devon |
| GREEN | The potter's term for raw or unfired ware |
| GREENWARE | See *Ware* |
| GROG | Powdered fired clay fabric, added to an unfired clay to improve its firing properties |
| GULLYMOUTH | See *Pitcher* |
| HAM PAN | A large oval or pear-shaped pot in which whole ham could be placed for salting. These usually had wooden lids, pierced for ventilation |
| HEN AND CHICKENS | A variety of money box decorated with small birds |
| HOG POT | A cylindrical jar used to salt pork joints |
| HOLLOW-WARE | Any deep vessels, such as jugs, cups or mugs |
| INCISING | Scratching decorative motifs into the surface of the pot |
| INLAYING | An ornamental technique in which a contrasting clay is rubbed into incised or stamped hollows in the fabric |
| IRON OXIDE | The oxide most commonly used by the potters to stain their glazes varying tones of brown |
| JOGGLING | A technique of slip decoration in which parallel |

lines of slip are first trailed across an area of contrasting wet slip over the fabric; the whole piece is then twisted and jerked to run the slip into a series of waves and swirls

JOLLY-BOYS — A Somerset and north Devon fuddling cup

KNIFE BOX — A pottery version of the wooden cutlery boxes made in the form of a deep tray with a raised slab cross-handle

KNIFE POT — A pot made either on the wheel or in slabs in which the cutlery is stored vertically

KNIFE TRIMMING — Trimming the foot of a vessel by paring away any surplus clay with a knife

LADING POT — A cylindrical pot of about ½gal capacity, with a large single handle. Used in northern England to bale water from the boiler to the washtub or bath

LEAD GLAZE — Lead formed a major part of all country potters' glazes, being used in the form of the oxide (litharge) or sulphide (galena)

LOVING CUP 1. A two-handled cup, usually in a semi-classical shape with a pedestal base and an inverted bell-shaped bowl. These cups were often used in nonconformist love-feasts during the late eighteenth and nineteenth centuries

2. An antiquarian and meaningless term for any cup with two handles

MARBLING — Superimposing slips of various colours over the green fabric and running them together either by shaking, or by the use of a sharp point or bristle to give a marbled finish (see also Joggling and Feathering)

MEAS CUP — A single-handed blackware mug made in Derbyshire or Yorkshire during the eighteenth and nineteenth centuries

MEAT DISH 1. From the sixteenth to the eighteenth century most meat dishes were rectangular trays some 12in by 18in and 3in deep, with two handles protruding from one of the long sides (see *Medieval Archaeology*, 8 [1964], 209)

2. Later meat dishes were usually in the form of a shallow pressed-ware tray, similar to baking dishes

OVENS 1. Bread ovens were made in Devon and Cornwall

from the early post-medieval period up to the mid-1930s. In shape they resemble large round beehives with closely fitting doors cut into their front faces

2. The Dutch oven of northern England or the apple roasters of Somerset were made from half a large cylindrical pan, with a narrow shelf formed round their internal curved walls and handles or knobs applied to their outer convex surfaces

OWL — A term used in the south and south west to describe a costrel with an almost spherical body and two pierced lugs near the neck, these features giving it an owl-like appearance

OWLSHEAD — A round-bodied redware pot used in Devon and Cornwall to prepare whiting

OXIDATION — The firing of a pot in an oxygen-rich atmosphere wherein the metallic elements in the clay are brought to their oxidised state, for instance, an iron-rich clay will burn to a red colour when oxidised, but will turn dark grey if fired in a reducing atmosphere, where there is no available oxygen

PAINT POT — A pot, rather like a chamber pot in shape, used by wheelwrights, house painters and so on, they gripped it in their left hands, inserting the thumb through the small loop handle and supporting the body with the palm of the hand, thus leaving the other hand free to wield the brush

PAN — A shortened form of 'pancheon'(?) an open straight-sided pottery vessel. In Devon these were classified according to size, growing from widebottoms to cawderns, bigpans and, largest of all, washpans

PANCHEON — An open vessel with straight-sided walls, usually splaying out to a rolled rim. It was mainly used for baking or washing purposes

PARTING CUP — A romantic antiquarian term, totally misleading, given to all multi-handled cups

PARTING SHERD — A small piece of broken pottery placed between various pots in the kiln to prevent them sticking together when the glaze melted

| | |
|---|---|
| PEELING | See *Flaking* |
| PIG | Hollow pottery pigs with removable heads were made in nineteenth-century Sussex, so enabling wedding guests to drink 'a hogshead' at the wedding feast. Pigs also acted as models for money boxes, probably because they suggested thrift, no part of a pig being without its use |
| PIGGIN | A shallow cylindrical pot with a flat handle extending vertically above the rim, thus copying the form of the cooper-made baler |
| PILCHARD POT | See *Bussa* |
| PILL | A costrel (particularly one from the Verwood pottery) used in Hampshire, Wiltshire and Dorset |
| PINCHGUT | See *Pitcher* |
| PITCHER | A south-country term for a jug. In north Devon pitchers are classified as: Pinchguts 4pt; Gullymouths $5\frac{1}{2}$pt; Thirtytales 7pt; Long Toms 2gal |
| PLANT POT | A straight-sided vessel, normally unglazed, with a drainage hole in the base, like the modern product |
| PORK-PAN | A deep pan with vertical sides used for salting pork. This term is used mainly in the south |
| POSSET POT | A pot, often bearing a lid, two handles and a spout, used to drink posset, a hot drink of milk flavoured with wine, ale, treacle, honey or spices |
| POTTLE | A 4pt pot |
| QUILL STRINGING | A Halifax term for slip-trailing |
| REDUCED GREENWARE | See *Ware* |
| REDUCTION | The process of firing a kiln in such a way that the gasses passing through the firing chamber are smoky and incompletely burnt. The carbon present during this operation reduces the metallic oxides within the clay and glaze to their metallic form, so that an iron-rich clay, for example, will fire to a dark-grey colour when reduced, instead of the normal bright-red oxidised colour |
| REDWARE | See *Ware* |
| RHUBARB POT | A large bottomless pot over 1ft in height and |

| | |
|---|---|
| | diameter, domed over at the top to leave a hole about 6in in diameter which is covered by a separate lid. The pot is placed over the rhubarb plant to 'force' it |
| RIB | A template of wood, metal or pottery used to finish a pot to a definite silhouette when it is thrown on the wheel |
| ROULETTING | The decoration of a pot by impressing it with a roller stamp, such as is used on butter-pats |
| SALTER | A north Devon term for an oval meat-salting pan |
| SALT KIT | A jar, completely domed over to a finial knob, with a circular hand-hole covered by a broad hood cut into its shoulder. In use in the north it hangs against a wall to hold cooking salt, which it is reputed to keep dry |
| SCALING | See *Flaking* |
| SEAKALE POT | A pot similar to a rhubarb pot in shape, used to force seakale mainly in the south from the mid-nineteenth century |
| SGRAFFITO | A technique of slip decoration in which a coating of slip is carefully scratched away when almost dry to reveal a contrasting colour of fabric beneath |
| SHERDS | Broken pieces of pottery |
| SLIP | Clay dissolved in water to the consistency of thick cream |
| SLIPWARE | See *Ware* |
| SNAIL-HORN WARE | A Halifax term for agate ware |
| SPITTOON | Open bowls filled with sawdust, used mainly in public houses where spitting frequently followed ale and chewed tobacco |
| SPOON | A north Devon term for a *rib* |
| SPRIG | A moulded detail of decoration applied to the green pot |
| SPURS | Clay tripods on which pots were often supported when being fired in the kiln |
| STAMPING | The impression of designs into the plastic clay by means of seal-like intaglios |
| STINK POT | See *Fuming Pot* |
| STONEWARE | See *Ware* |
| STOUKING | A Staffordshire term for affixing the handles, |

lugs, spouts and so on to the body of the pots (see Dr Plot's *History of Staffordshire* of 1686)

SULPHATION — The formation of white or yellowish patches on the surface of the glaze caused by sulphur in the fuel or in the glaze. In a normal well-ventilated through-draught kiln this trouble was rare, but it was common where galena glazes were fired in closed saggers or in electric kilns

TENMOKU — A black glaze often shot with streaks of rust colour. Although this glaze is best known in the stonewares of Japan, the same glazing results were occasionally and apparently accidentally achieved on high-fired redwares in England

TERRACOTTA — Fine unglazed redware, mainly used for architectural details and garden ornaments

THIRTYTALES — See *Pitcher*

THROWING — Process of shaping pots on the potter's wheel

TRAILING — A method of slip decoration in which coloured slips are piped on to greenwares through a fine nozzle

TURNING — Trimming the walls or base of a pot with a chisel-edged blade as it spins on the potter's wheel

TYG — An ornamental mug, frequently decorated with slip-trailing and applied pads of clay, with a number of highly ornate handles which are often hollow, concealing drinking spouts

WARE — Pottery in general, or a specific variety, such as:

*Agate ware* — A fabric made of clays of two or more colours which have been coarsely mixed to produce a marble-like effect (not to be confused with marbling, a *surface* decoration in slip)

*Bargee-ware* — A type of pottery made in the late nineteenth and early twentieth centuries which had a red fabric ornamented with sprigs of white clay and dabs of Wenger's colours. So called from its popularity with the bargees of the midlands waterways

*Blackware* — Earthenwares, usually with a red fabric, glazed with a dense black lead glaze

| | |
|---|---|
| *Brownware* | This term has been used by various writers to describe:<br>1. a redware glazed to a brown colour<br>2. a stoneware glazed with salt to a warm brown-orange-peel finish |
| *Earthenware* | Pottery with a porous fabric, fired to about 1,000°C |
| *Greenware* | Pottery made from an earthenware fabric which fires to a cream colour due to its iron-free state, and which has been given a lead glaze stained to a brilliant green with copper |
| *Reduced Greenware* | Redware (see below) fired in a reducing atmosphere with little or no oxygen, to produce a slate-grey colour. This appears olive-green beneath a yellow tinted lead glaze |
| *Redware* | Pottery made from a red-firing earthenware fabric, fired in an oxygen-rich atmosphere. It is often glazed to an orange, brown or black by the use of lead glazes |
| *Slipware* | Pottery decorated with slips |
| *Stoneware* | Pottery which is impervious to water, vitrifying at temperatures usually in excess of 1,200°C |
| *Welsh-ware* | Slipware of extremely high quality, usually with a white fabric and bright-coloured slips, often with complex feathered and sgraffito decoration |
| *White-ware* | Pottery made from a white-firing earthenware fabric, and normally made only in pottery factories |
| *Yellow-ware* | Pottery made from a yellow to buff-firing fabric, often appearing butter-coloured under a lead glaze |

WASH PAN — See *Pan*

WATCH-POCKET — A pottery mantelpiece ornament, frequently bearing lively modelled decoration, which has a small pocket applied to its back surface into which a watch may be placed so that its face fills a round aperture on the front of the piece; mainly nineteenth-century in date

WHISTLE — Small pottery whistles were made in many eighteenth- and nineteenth-century potteries in the north, many of them being given away to the children of prospective customers to attract their parents. Larger whistles, in the form of pigeons in bowers, were also made from the early nineteenth century onwards, bird-calls being made when the base of their tails are softly blown

| | |
|---|---|
| WIDEBOTTOM | See *Pan* |
| YELLOW-WARE | See *Ware* |

# *Bibliography*

For further information regarding individual potteries and potters the reader is recommended to consult the companion volume *The English Country Pottery, its History and Techniques,* published in 1971. Further information and illustrative material concerning country pottery may be obtained from the following:


Baines, J. M. *Sussex Pottery* (Hastings 1948)

Barton, K. J. 'Buckley Potteries 2, Excavations at Prescot's Pottery', *Flintshire Hist Soc Publications,* 16 (1956), 63–87

Bemrose, G. *Nineteenth Century English Pottery and Porcelain* (1952)

Bourne, G. *William Smith, Potter and Farmer, 1790–1858* (1920)

Bradley, R. J. *Castle Hedingham Pottery, 1837–1905* (1968)

Brears, P. C. D. *Catalogue of the English Country Pottery Housed in the Yorkshire Museum, York* (1968); 'Techniques of the Truro Pottery', *Folk Life,* 10 (1972), 47–54; and *The Farnham Potteries* (Farnham 1971)

Chaffers, W. *Marks and Monograms on Pottery and Porcelain* (1863)

Church, Sir A. *English Earthenware* (1885)

Cooper, R. G. *English Slipware Dishes, 1650–1850* (1968)

Crawley, J. *The Potteries of Sunderland and District* (Sunderland 1961)

Douch, H. L. 'Cornish Earthenware Potters', *Journal of the Royal Institution of Cornwall,* New Series 6, part 1 (1969)

English Ceramic Circle *Proceedings* (1933 to date)

Grabham, O. *Yorkshire Potteries, Pots, and Potters* (1916)

Haggar, R. G. 'Country Pottery and Porcelain', *Concise Encyclopedia of Antiques,* 2 (1955); and *English Country Pottery* (1950)

Hobson, R. L. *Catalogue of the Collection of English Pottery in the British Museum* (1903)

Hodgkin, J. E. and E. *Early English Pottery with Names and Dates* (1891); and *Examples of Early English Pottery* (1896)
Holland, W. F. *Fifty Years a Potter* (1958)
Honey, W. B. *English Pottery and Porcelain,* revised by R. J. Charleston (1962)
Hughes, G. B. *Victorian Pottery and Porcelain* (1959)
Jewitt, L. *The Ceramic Art of Great Britain* (1878)
Kenworthy, J. *The Midhope Potteries* (Sheffield 1928)
Kleyn, J. de. *Volksaardewerk in Nederland 1600–1900* (N. V. Zeist 1965)
Leach, B. *A Potter's Book* (1945)
Leicester Museums. *A Catalogue of the Permanent Collection of English Ceramics* (Leicester 1953)
Lewis, G. *A Picture History of English Pottery* (1956)
Lomax, C. *Quaint Old English Pottery* (1909)
Parkinson, M. R. *The Incomparable Art* (Manchester 1969); *Post-Medieval Archaeology* (1967 to date)
Rackham, B. *Catalogue of the Glaisher Collection in the Fitzwilliam Museum, Cambridge* (1935); and *Early Staffordshire Pottery* (1951)
Rackham, B. and Rhead, H. *English Pottery* (1924)
Reeks, T. and Ruddler, F. W. *British Pottery and Porcelain in the Museum of Practical Geology,* 2nd edn (1971)
Rhead, G. W. and F. A. *Staffordshire Pots and Potters* (1906)
Savage, G. *English Pottery and Porcelain* (1961)
Sidebotham, Dr. *Catalogue of the Greg Collection of English Pottery now in the City Art Gallery, Manchester* (1923)
Solon, M. L. *The Art of the Old English Potter* (1885)
Taggart, R. E. *The Frank P. and Harriet C. Burnap Collection of English Pottery,* 2nd edn (Kansas 1967)
Walton, J. 'Some Decadent Local Industries', *Halifax Antiquarian Society Transactions,* 19 (1939)
Watkins, C. M. 'North Devon Pottery and Its Export to America in the Seventeenth Century', *United States National Museum Bulletin,* 225 (Washington 1960)
Wedgwood, J. C. and Ormsbee T. H. *Staffordshire Pottery* (1947)

# *Acknowledgements*

The compilation of this volume has involved extensive visits to museums, art galleries and libraries throughout England where, without exception, the author has been given the greatest possible assistance. Access to reserve collections and the occasional closed gallery has always been granted by helpful staff who, although too numerous to mention individually, each deserve the author's most sincere thanks.

A special debt is also owed to the potters who have patiently answered countless questions regarding the wares formerly and currently made in their potteries, including Mr G. Curtis of Littlethorpe, Messrs A. and R. Harris of Farnham, Mr W. Lake of Truro, Mr H. Thorburn of Weatheriggs, Mr R. Bateson of Burton-in-Lonsdale, the late Mr I. Button of Halifax and the late Mr W. F. Holland, formerly of Fremington.

The author is also extremely grateful to the various institutions and individuals who have kindly given their permission to reproduce items from their respective collections. These are acknowledged in the List of Illustrations.

Peter C. D. Brears

# Index